Atelophobia
(a-tel-o-pho-bia)
The Fear Of Imperfection
Extended

Nakida Parker-Coore

Atelophobia Extended Version

NSpired Thinking Publishing, LLC
info@nspiredthinking.com
For information, please visit our Web site at
www.nspiredthinking.com
NSpired Thinking Publishing, LLC and its logo are registered trademarks.

PUBLISHER'S NOTE

Without limiting the rights under the copyright reserved above, no part of this publication may be reproduced, stored in or introduced into a retrieval system, or transmitted, in any form, or by any means (electronic, mechanical, photocopying, recording, or otherwise), without the prior written permission of both the copyright owner and the above publisher of this book.

Atelophobia
By Nakida Parker-Coore
Copyright © Nakida Parker-Coore, 2014, 2017
All Rights Reserved.
ISBN: 978-0999366226
E book: 978-0999366233
Second Edition.
Printed in the USA.

Note From The Author:

The Hardest thing for a perfectionist is having a baby, nurturing it, letting it go out into the world and then being told it wasn't good enough. Atelophobia was and still is my baby but I decided to create an extended edition in order to explain the story in more depth for my readers and then I will be moving on from McKenzie and her journey. For now. No, it's not because of one bad review, it is because I have focused on her and stayed stagnant for 3 years because her story is extremely personal to me but I have a lot more to tell. I want to thank all of the readers that purchased the original edition and enjoyed it. I want to also thank you all for your patience with me. I am not kidding when I say the fear of imperfection is REAL for me.

I want to thank my parents Steve and Chante Austin, my brother Navaughn, my children: Jeremiah, Chase and Tyler for the motivation. I also have to thank my readers, my husband Andre, my sisters Nyghea and Ebony. My cousins Kalilah and Amanze, My friends Asia, Emely, Taylor, Malayna, Shedeen, Tamara, Tiffany, Zuley and of course I have to thank My Yai Yai. Some of you have spent time with me on the book, some have pushed me to move forward and stop letting fear get in the way. Some have reminded me of the support I have, some have also reminded me that I am enough and as time goes on I will get even better.

Rest in Peace Dad (Steve Austin) I love you always.

"Your imperfections are marks of authenticity, and that is the beauty of you."

-Isaac Fowler

Introduction:

During a discussion about life, a wise woman told me "Behind every face there is a story." I believe her wholeheartedly; no one around me knows details about who I am, what I go through, what I have been through and how it molded me into the person I am today. I have always felt like I was not good enough because people are quick to judge a book by its cover before taking the time to actually read the book. So, I figured "they", meaning whoever; could only judge me from what they see on the surface. They could not judge me or talk about me based on what I was facing emotionally. I always felt like people would think my emotions were dumb or not important.

Growing up, I was the girl with the attitude, because I did not walk around with a smile on my face. In my opinion, only clowns walked around smiling. But, that's neither here nor there. I was the girl who was quick to tell someone about themselves for messing with a family member or friend but I'd rarely defend myself.

Growing up, I yearned for someone I could talk to without being judged for what came out of my mouth or how it came out of my mouth. I yearned for someone I could explain my feelings to. I wanted someone, anyone to understand why I was angry and stand off-ish. But, I felt like there was no one who could complete that job.

Now that I think about it, I feel like that is just a lack of trust. Most people start out giving people chances. Someone will give a person 100 percent then the person might decrease that trust level as time goes on, but for me? It did not quite happen that way.
I was afraid to be close to my family because of how they

talked about me and each other. I was afraid to have friends because I was told family would never let me down and that is all they have done. I was unable to keep a relationship because I was unable to trust that they wouldn't hurt me, before the person even messed up. I'm not sure I know how to love properly because the people I thought I was showing love to did not show the same love back.

    Personally, I don't mind admitting that I long for acceptance more than anything else on this earth. Shit, who doesn't? Even the people who say they do not want to be or do not care to be. Because I never thought I was good enough, I felt like I was never accepted by the people who were the most important to me. Of course that statement would be up for debate if those people heard me saying this. But, my perception IS in fact, my reality. In my reality, some of these people knew me my whole life but still would not know the difference between me and their neighbor. I wish they would have gotten to know me better so maybe if they did not love me, they would have learned how to.

    My mother and my grandmother have been trying to get me to come here for as long as I can remember. I don't want to live the rest of my life in an unhappy state of mind. So, I agreed because I am really hoping this works. I am ready to move on.

    "McKenzie? Perkins?" The receptionist called my name; I walked over to the window at a slow pace.

    "Yes?" I responded to her, and she looked up and smiled. I noticed her name on her name tag. "I apologize, I didn't introduce myself earlier. Hi Tori."

    "Hi McKenzie, you looked a little distracted when you came over to check in initially. I didn't want to bother you." she responded with a smile.

    "Yes, I was. But I'm okay now."

    "First time?" she asked.

    "Yes, First time for everything I suppose." I responded

with a snicker.

"You'll love her. Mrs. Williams will be waiting for you down the hall, her door is the last one on the left side."

The therapist is ready to see me.

Atelophobia Extended Version

Cousins:

I walked down the hall towards Mrs. Williams office. It was a very quiet and clean environment. The black and white photography on the walls made the hall look beautiful, and the marble floors put the icing on the cake. I found her name on the door I was looking for; it was cracked so I knocked first.

"McKenzie?" Jodi called. I peeped my head into the room and waved.

"Yes, it's me. May I come in?" I asked.

"Yes! You are who I have been waiting to see." Jodi stood up from the black sofa where she was reading her book, and I realized how young she was. I can honestly say I was expecting an old woman with glasses. She looked like she was no older than in her late 30s. She did wear glasses; I was right on that one. She had pretty, long brown hair, with a slim figure. Jodi kind of reminded me of a new grade school teacher, fresh out of college.

"I hope I didn't interrupt you at the good part." I joked.

"Oh, don't worry about it. I was just catching up on a James Patterson book. This one is titled The Quickie, and it is hard to put down! Do you like to read?" Jodi asked with enthusiasm. I was glad we already had something in common. She sat back down on the sofa after putting her book on the desk and picking up her notepad and pen.

"Reading is my favorite hobby. I wish I had more me time to enjoy it."

"Life can be demanding, but you have to make sure you make time for what you enjoy." She responded.

I nodded my head and sat next to Jodi on the sofa. I was a little nervous, but she helped me warm up a bit.

"So, tell me about yourself before we get started. Plus,

add in your favorite color and your biggest fear." Ice Breakers, everyone uses them. It's so cliché.

"Well, I'm McKenzie my last name is Perkins. I am a mother of two boys: a four-year-old and an infant. I graduated from the University of New Haven with a Bachelors Degree in business marketing. I am a Realtor and a wholesale investor. I am 23 years old, I moved to Connecticut at the age of 13; I used to live in the Manhattan borough of New York City. I love reading and writing, and my biggest fear is death." Jodi smiled, nodded her head, and began to tell me about herself.

"So, my name is Jodi Williams, as you know. I am 37 years old, a mother of a boy, Tyler, and a girl, Taylor. Tyler is seven and Taylor is five. I've been married for 10 years; I graduated from NYU; I was born and raised in Greenwich, CT, I am deathly afraid of spiders, and my favorite hobbies are reading and working out."

I checked Jodi's figure out, I see how her hobby is keeping her in great shape.

"Since this is our first session, we have two hours. Within these two hours, we will be getting to know one another and figuring out what we will be working on. Going forward it will only be a one-hour session. So, McKenzie, what brings you here?" I really did not know where to begin.

"Well, I guess I can start with trust issues. I trust almost no one."

"Where did it begin?" Jodi asked.

I believe that you learn your first lessons from your family members. As a kid, I learned that family could actually be the first people to hurt you if and when they can. When the people in my family were the ones to hurt me, in my experience, it hurt the most because they are my blood and I expected more. Family members are supposed to love each other and be there for one another not hurt each other. That is how I was raised anyway, we were always taught not to let anyone "on the outside" harm us and we are supposed to protect one another. As I started to learn things on my own, I learned that is not always the case. Not with the Daniel's or the Perkin's anyway.

For as long as I can remember, I have always had a hard time making friends with females. I could not stand humans with body parts like mine, with an exception of a few. Those few were later in life though. I was born into my own group of friends. Really, they were my cousins, Brittany, Kyle, and Tiffany. They are a part of my mother's side of my family, The Daniels. They were my favorite people right along with Junior and Sean. Sean, Junior and I shared the same grandmother they were hardly around all of us but my mom had them from time to time and so did our Nana Christina.

I was the tomboy out of the three girls. Maybe that was the reason I was so close to the boys. Kyle is like a big brother to me; he was the guy you wanted to grow up and be like when you were younger. Kyle played basketball, so I played basketball. Kyle liked Pokémon and as much as I did not understand it, I "liked" Pokémon and the list goes on.

Tiffany is cool, though we never were really close. I am unsure why; we never clicked, but I don't love her any less than I do the others. I always wanted to be cool with her the way Brittany was, but it just never happened for us.

I was pretty close to Brittany, but we fought as if we were sisters. It was a love-hate relationship between us. Our first fight I will never forget, ever.

"One day, my cousins and I were out all night and morning with our uncle Thomas. He took us to the Apollo, and of course I was up under Kyle most of the time. For some reason, that caused an issue between Brittany and I.

When we got back to our great-grandmother's house, she picked a fight with me. She decided to tell me how she really felt, I suppose. She said I acted like a boy and that is the reason why Tiffany liked her more than she liked me. We were young at the time, I had to be about 7 years old, which made her about 9." Jodi looked up from her note pad once I stopped talking.

"So, Jessica just randomly felt a way about you hanging with Kyle?" Jodi asked with clear confusion on her face.

"Well, I'm not sure. But, the way that things played out. That is the way it seemed."

"Was that the only argument the two of you had?" She asked, and I smirked.

"No, that day we got into our fist fight and other days we argued over stupid things."

Jodi shook her head in dismay, not that I can blame her. We were two young kids fighting for no reason.

"Kyle and Tiffany broke that fight up, and somehow my great-grandmother got wind of it and told us to come into her room. That was the first time we got "the speech," she reminded us we are family we should be protecting each other from people on the streets and not fighting each other. As a kid, I was optimistic. Although I heard every single word she said, and I will never forget how it made me feel, I was still hoping we would go back to how we were before the fight. I thought maybe she was just upset. But the fighting was consistent, annoying to be quite honest! What hurts me the most is that, still to this day I really don't know what her problem is with me."

I know that our elders had their own issues with one another but I don't see how Brittany and I have anything to do with it. We always had to beg for Brittany to sleep over at our house. It felt like my aunt Jackie forbade her to be near us. Years went on and eventually we just gave up, but Brittany's behavior got worse, which ended up bringing us back together. She began stressing my aunt Jackie out and my mother came to her rescue.

"Brittany came to live with us and my parents took care

of her every need with no help from anyone else. Brittany had everything she wanted and needed. From clothing on her back to food in her stomach, she did everything with me, and we all were treated equally. She truly was my parents' fourth child at that time.

"People with a heart would appreciate things like that. Well, I would appreciate if my older cousin decided to add me to her family. I would appreciate and respect my cousin forever because she did what no one else did for me and she did what she didn't have to do. But, that's where Brittany and I were different.

"As years passed, I began to notice things I didn't agree with about her: the disrespect she had for our cousin Jackson because he was *different* to say the least; the way she was able to talk to adults or the way she was able to get away with being mean to other kids, and all we heard was "You know better, so act like it!" That wasn't fair then, and it isn't fair now. We were all brought up the same way, respecting each other and our elders, so why weren't these rules embedded in everyone?"

Jodi disrupted my thoughts with a question.

"Was your relationship with Brittany all bad? Or did the bad just outweigh all of the good?" I thought back to the good times.

"I remember making up dances for birthday parties with my cousins, and the times when everyone would pile up at my mom's, and we would have sleepovers. Family, friends, and church family. I mean, almost every kid you can think of came. Those days were the best. We were a small family but we always made the best out of that. Our family always fake adopted other people into our family. My mom adopted two; I have a god sister named Victoria now, and an older sister named Jessica."

Victoria went away from us, got married, and only really hangs with her husband. We don't really get to see her too much these days. As for Jessica, she may have needed space but she never really left. It doesn't matter how much Jessica and I fight, argue, disagree, and agree, I know she always has my back. She isn't judgmental, and she doesn't think she's better; she's just a good person to me. Everyone was close to Jessica. She went to my aunt Lisa's church with her family and everyone basically grew up with her as well as I did. I have heard stories about her being a bad teenager, but I'm not the judgmental type. I was a kid at the time, so I felt and still feel it has absolutely nothing to do with me.

As I aged, I was able to be in adult conversations without getting into trouble. I learned a couple of things about Uncle David and Jessica's relationship. I always heard that they were dating, even with their awkward age gap; and that she was cheating on him. Uncle David was the only boy out of my great-grand mother's six kids, and he was the baby, so everyone was sensitive to what was going on in his life. Sometimes, I wondered if his siblings exaggerated what happened with him or was it the truth. I feel like I can't take what they say at face value because they are extremely over protective.

I was 19 years old when I found out I was pregnant with my oldest son Tahj. The whole family had something negative to say about it except my great-grandmother, and, of course, Kyle. Kyle always believed in me and I'll never forget what my great-grandmother told me.

"I was a young mother too, suga. We all make mistakes. Nothing to be sorry about, and with or without the father you will be fine."

My experience with other family members wasn't as reassuring. I remember Brittany writing me on AIM telling me that Tiffany told her she doesn't want to end up like me. Looking back, I don't think she was trying to hurt me. But, it did. I also remember my aunt Lisa yelling at me at the top of her lungs, and my Nana mentioning an abortion, something I personally do not believe in. Jessica and Kyle, on the other hand, never mentioned anything negative to me. All I needed was support, and that's what they provided. I cannot stress how much I appreciate them. They knew I didn't need bashing, and that's why I would never turn my back on Kyle or Jessica. When I needed someone the most, they were there.

One day, my family decided to call a meeting. My mother had gotten the scoop on what the meeting was about from my Nana Christina. So, I knew details before we headed down to Manhattan and I also knew I did not want anything to do with this meeting.
"What was the meeting about?" Jodi asked.

"Well, apparently my family believed Jessica was stealing from my Nana's brother; uncle David, who was sick at the time. They wanted everyone to stop speaking to h er. You know, the blood is thicker than water thing." Jodi smirked and nodded her head.

"I just figured why should I? The day of the meeting came and went, and no, I did not cut Jessica off. Like I said, I wouldn't. No one in my house did." I continued.

After walking into the house and taking a seat in the living room, it was hard not to notice the tension. I sat on the couch at my great-grandmother's house while Sharon put Tahj in the back for a nap. Everyone came in, took a seat and waited for the meeting to begin. I noticed almost all of my cousins, aunts and uncles attended the meeting. The only people who were absent were: Uncle David, my late aunt Jackie, Kyle and Tiffany; they were away on a business trip together. Four of uncle David's siblings were there including all of their kids. My mother's brother Michael even came from Buffalo New York, which was rare so I knew this, was serious.

"Hey Family, how's everybody?" My aunt Lisa asked. Everyone replied that they were doing well and she began.

"Well, I wanted to have a meeting today about your Uncle David, and Jessica. We all know my brother is very ill, and it has been brought to my attention that Jessica is taking advantage of him.

She handed out pieces of paper, which appeared to be copies of his bank statements. Here we fucking go.

Death Of The Family:

I looked down at the bank statements, and I noticed money transfers, which meant absolutely nothing to me because according to these adults, he had been paying her for years to "be" with him before she turned eighteen years old. So, in my opinion, they weren't showing me anything I should have been upset about, but I kept my mouth quiet and kept my ears open. I was just waiting for someone, anyone, to elaborate on the situation at hand.

Of course that elaboration came from aunt Lisa.

"Well, we know they had an ugly break up and despite whatever went wrong, Jessica offered to assist with his care taking. Which now I see, was a bad idea. Christina and I went to the bank because our brother wanted us to take over his account. The transactions listed on the paper you have in front of you, did not sit right with us. We confirmed with David that he hadn't approved these transactions, so we proceeded to speak with the bank teller about their security procedures."

I listened to my aunt explain the story, and I instantly became angry. Uncle David has a lot wrong with him. To my knowledge, he hardly remembered anything, so I didn't understand why anyone was taking his word for it. I mean, no disrespect to my uncle, but I wouldn't believe all of what he said, but that was just me.

"Jessica has been stealing money from your Uncle David. This is one of the biggest betrayals to our family and we cannot just let this slide." Aunt Lisa continued. I began to hear Brittany make small comments in the middle of my aunt talking. At that point, I knew the meeting wasn't going to be about Uncle David and Jessica for much longer.

"Aren't we supposed stick together? If the family is against someone, aren't we all supposed to be against the person too? How come SOME people are able to still talk to our enemy?" Brittany was coming for me, indirectly, of course. I simply looked at my mother, and we smiled at each other.

"Well, who are you talking about? Because her daughter is my godchild, and I will always be there for her even though I am pissed off at her mother," my aunt retorted.

Brittany refused to look at me but she just repeated herself. "Some people just shouldn't be talking to her, that's all."

"Well, I'm grown I can make my own decisions and I will always speak to Jessica. She's my sons godmother, and on top of that, she was there for me when you all were not. When I was expecting Tahj, what support did I get from any of you? But, yet you mentioned, sticking together? " My mother interrupted me.

"There's nothing to argue about Kenz, leave it alone. We came here to discuss Uncle David and Jessica, you don't have to explain yourself to her. I am your mother." My mom turned and faced the front of the room. "Carry on Aunt Lisa."

Brittany's face turned red, she became angry with my mother now. I figured it was because of the way she was dismissed. My mother is known for her dismissals. I looked towards Aunt Lisa but she was staring at Brittany, as if she was waiting for the explosion. I looked over at Brit and she began to yell. She started screaming how fake she thought my mother and I were for keeping Jessica in our lives. I was very calm; I wasn't reacting to anything she said, which may have scared my mother. I figured I should keep my cool because It seems like it's not about Jessica being in our lives, there is something she has been holding in. Once I tried to speak, I was told to "shut up" by my elders anyway.

Finally, I asked my mother why is it okay for Brittany to speak and not me, why is everyone always jumping to her defense during every incident that she causes and not mine? My cousin Asia stood up and so did my mother, Asia stood in front of Brittany and my mother stood in front of me. Asia was a few years younger than my mom, she was my mothers peer. I kept hearing Brittany screaming and the only thing stopping me from shutting her up myself was our older cousin Tara, who was sitting in between us. I had so much respect for my older cousins and the elders in the room, I wouldn't dare put my hands on Brittany in front of them.

As soon as Asia and my mother walked away, Brittany jumped up and attempted to get in my face. My uncle Michael grabbed her and asked her to be quiet.

"Shut the fuck up," Brittany hissed at Michael. I don't have to listen to you." I marveled that she was always allowed to be so disrespectful. He didn't even say anything back other than "be quiet."

"Don't talk to my uncle like that! Watch your fuckin' mouth," I screamed back, and aunt Lisa tried to play mediator. Brittany started screaming and yelling again and some of our family members decided to try and bring her out the house.

While my aunts and cousins were attempting to take Brittany out the house, I heard her scream, "I wish I could get to you, I would fuck you up."

From where she was standing, I noticed she had to be talking to my mother, and I blacked out.

"I mean, honestly Jodi," I said, coming back to the present. "Who would allow someone to threaten his or her mother? Family or not, cousin, brother, sister, I don't care. I couldn't deal with it."

Jodi nodded her head in agreement. "I don't agree with violence, but I can definitely understand why you reacted that way."

"It was like, out of all people she was the last person I'd expect to be so damn ungrateful. I was not expecting that at all, I didn't even know she had an issue with my mother in the first place. "

I noticed I had begun to finish my thought, as if Jodi wasn't even in the room. That memory took me back to a dark place and even now every time I think about it, I feel the same way.

"It hurts really bad when you do not know why someone always has so much hostility towards you. I am almost twenty-four years old and I have not found out what the real issue was. We were only children when this started, what could I have done to her at 7 years old?"

"In a situation like this, where someone never openly expresses what their issue is with you. There is not much you can do about it. You can ask Brittany if there is a way for the two of you to resolve the issue. You can bring her here if you like, so that I can mediate. Just keep in mind, if it does not work, you did what you could. So, what happened after the incident at your Great-Grand mothers house? I'm guessing it was swept under the rug?" Jodi asked, and I began to think back to that day.

"It's okay, she's just like that, and you should know better than her, Kenzie." Aunt Samantha is one of Uncle David's sisters, a long with aunt Lisa and my nana Christina. Usually aunt Samantha is the quiet one out of the bunch, and at that moment I wish she had stayed that way.

"It's always been okay for her to act crazy," I said, exasperated.

"Even when we were kids, I would come to any one of you, and I would hear the same thing; 'She's different'. But if my two-year-old son knows right from wrong, so should she! I'm tired of hearing excuses! Brittany disrespecting my mother was way over the top! My mom didn't have to do anything for her but she did everything and asked for nothing in return. Ms. Britt has a few birthdays, suddenly she's grown and thinks it is okay to be disrespectful?"

I remember crying from frustration at this point. I couldn't believe it; I was in total disgust with my whole family. From that point on, I knew I had to keep my distance. Things would never be fair between the family and I and to keep the peace I should stay away. I finally gave up.

Shortly after that, maybe a week or two later, I called my Nana to see how she was doing. She told me she was on her way to Uncle David's house because he hadn't been answering the phone and she was nervous. I stayed on the phone with her until she arrived at his house.

"Well, why is the door open?" Nana said out loud, I could hear the concern in her voice. She suddenly became really quiet before telling me she would call me back, and without her giving me any details I knew Uncle David was no longer with us.

"I'm sorry for your loss" Jodi said.

"Thank you, I actually cried that time. I was a little numb that last year when aunt Jackie passed away but with him, I'm honestly not sure why I cried. I expected it; it wasn't a surprise, but my feelings were still hurt. I just knew at that very moment it was not just the death of my uncle David, it was the death of the Daniels family."

"Remember McKenzie, you must first ask the questions you want answers to. There has to be a reason that there is so much animosity between you and Brittany, and there must be a reason behind people sticking up for Brittany the way they do. Are you willing to take the necessary steps, to find out exactly what is going on here?" Jodi asked.

"I would like to, but I don't think it would do any good." I asked her.

"So, you don't have anymore faith left in the Daniel's

Atelophobia Extended Version

future at all?" Jodi asked.

"I did have faith, until I arrived at Uncle David's funeral. It was the first time I seen my family since the blow out at my great-grand mothers house. No one really spoke; everyone was distant. Maybe people were still upset about the incident that took place, but it looked as if, it was my mom and me against my cousins. That sounds stupid, I know but it is what it is. Going forward from that day on, that's always how it has been: "us versus them". The funeral gave me confirmation that things may never be fair between us. The Daniel's will always take Brittany's side without considering mine. For now, I'm not interested in figuring anything out. Maybe, in the future Brittany and I can fix our relationship but right now, there are other things that I am focused on."

I told Jodi how Brittany was just a prime example of why I can't trust people. If I can't trust or get along with my own family, I don't see it happening with anyone else. When I moved to Connecticut at the age of 13, I was automatically on guard.

Starting over is never easy, especially being the new girl in a new school at my age. I always thought I would never leave Manhattan but I know my mother had to do what she had to do. A lot happened to me the first year and a half living in Connecticut. Sometimes, I wish I knew that this place was going to change my life forever. I watch a lot of television and I always hear the term "Fresh meat" when referring to freshman's. On television, all the upperclassmen are mean to the freshman's. Here at Hamden High it was the exact opposite, most of the upperclassmen are so friendly.

Almost everyone loved the new girl! Most of the boys wanted to do me, some who were too old claimed me as their little sister, that sort of thing was going on for a while.

"Did you make any friends?" Jodi asked.

"Yeah, I had more male friends than girls, but there

was Andrea, Lily, King, Ethan, Andrew, and a few others. King passed away not long after we met. That was the first death I had ever experienced in life."

"What happened to King?" Jodi asked.

My thoughts went back to the third week of attending Hamden High School, I remembered how excited I was. Waking up, I already knew exactly what I was going to wear. The first two weeks went by quickly, but they were perfect and I could not wait to start my day. I met a few people so far, but not everyone stood out. Lily and I met in first period on the first day of school. We had two more classes together throughout the day. We met Andrea during last period and the three of us instantly clicked. I hung out with Lily and Andrea three or four times after school, and Andrea introduced King to Lily and me. When I woke up, I originally intended on meeting up with Lily and Andrea before class. I was running a little late, so instead I headed straight to the cafeteria to grab breakfast instead of meeting with the girls.

"Kenzi! How are you?" I heard King yell to me. I was confused seeing him, because during a conversation when we met, he mentioned to me he was going to a different school.

"I'm okay, I thought you went to Norwalk High?"

"I do, shhh," he replied, using exaggerated gestures as if he really was trying to hide his true identity. I couldn't help but laugh as I walked away. King was always up to something.

"Talking on the phone with Andrea a few days after seeing King, we decided to give him a call."

Coming back to the present, I began to tell Jodi about the last conversation I had with King before we got the news that he was no longer with us.

"He seemed so much better than he actually was, apparently. He sounded so regular, telling us about his girlfriend problems, how he was into church, and how much he was enjoying his new baby sister. In the school hallway was the last time I saw him before putting him to rest and that phone call was the last time we spoke. The story behind his death puzzles me.

"It is puzzling to me because for King to be such a happy person during the short time I have known him, I would not have thought taking his own life was on his agenda. Losing King was the first time I experienced the death of someone I knew. The passing of my family members happened later in life.

"The day I found out, I met with Andrea, and we walked down to Kings house to meet a few people from school. His family was not home at the time, so we sat on his porch and cried for hours. It was some type of comfort, you know? He used to sit out front all the time, so it felt like he was with us. We sat out there and reminisced about everything, from when each of us first met him until the last day we spoke to him."

"How did he pass away?" Jodi asked.

"He shot himself." I looked away as Jodi began to write something in her notepad.

"I'm sorry for your loss," she responded, "At a young age, in a new state, I can only imagine how traumatizing it may have been to go through that."

I looked out the window and my thoughts went back into that place.

"After King passed, it seems like nothing got better. I lost my virginity the following year, and my then on and off again boyfriend Ethan and I basically went to war after that."

Ethan and I began dating a month after King passed, we were always on and off. Only the Lord himself really knows why, but I was still positive that we would be together literally until "death do us part." That is how infatuated I was with him, and it was a very scary thing to feel in such a short period of time. Andrea was probably the only person who understood how much love I had for Ethan. Anything he did, whether it was right or wrong I'm always on his side. Even if something hurts me mentally or physically I will be his lawyer until the end, it was always him and me forever.

During the first year of our on and off relationship, Ethan was also on and off with many other females. It took me a whole year, standing by watching him do what he wants for me to finally decide to do what I wanted to do. Ethan told me on a drunk night he lost his virginity to an upperclassmen. I was only 13 years old, I was hurt and was not thinking rationally.

After finding out what he did, I kept Ethan in my life but I also kept some male friends around who were there when I needed them.

Turning Point:

"Remember McKenzie, you must first ask the questions you want answers to. There has to be a reason that there is so much animosity between you and Brittany, and there must be a reason behind people sticking up for Brittany the way they do. Are you willing to take the necessary steps, to find out exactly what is going on here?" Jodi asked.

"I would like to, but I don't think it would do any good." I asked her.

"So, you don't have anymore faith left in the Daniel's future at all?" Jodi asked.

"I did have faith, until I arrived at Uncle David's funeral. It was the first time I seen my family since the blow out at my great-grand mothers house. No one really spoke; everyone was distant. Maybe people were still upset about the incident that took place, but it looked as if, it was my mom and me against my cousins. That sounds stupid, I know but it is what it is. Going forward from that day on, that's always how it has been: "us versus them". The funeral gave me confirmation that things may never be fair between us. The Daniel's will always take Brittany's side without considering mine. For now, I'm not interested in figuring anything out. Maybe, in the future Brittany and I can fix our relationship but right now, there are other things that I am focused on."

I told Jodi how Brittany was just a prime example of why I can't trust people. If I can't trust or get along with my own family, I don't see it happening with anyone else. When I moved to Connecticut at the age of 13, I was automatically on guard.

Starting over is never easy, especially being the new girl

in a new school at my age. I always thought I would never leave Manhattan but I know my mother had to do what she had to do. A lot happened to me the first year and a half living in Connecticut. Sometimes, I wish I knew that this place was going to change my life forever.

I watch a lot of television and I always hear the term "Fresh meat" when referring to freshman's. On television, all the upperclassmen are mean to the freshman's. Here at Hamden High it was the exact opposite, most of the upperclassmen are so friendly. Almost everyone loved the new girl! Most of the boys wanted to do me, some who were too old claimed me as their little sister, that sort of thing was going on for a while.

"Did you make any friends?" Jodi asked.

"Yeah, I had more male friends than girls, but there was Andrea, Lily, King, Ethan, Andrew, and a few others. King passed away not long after we met. That was the first death I had ever experienced in life."

"What happened to King?" Jodi asked.

My thoughts went back to the third week of attending Hamden High School, I remembered how excited I was. Waking up, I already knew exactly what I was going to wear. The first two weeks went by quickly, but they were perfect and I could not wait to start my day. I met a few people, but not everyone stood out. Lily and I met in first period on the first day of school. We had two more classes together throughout the day. We met Andrea during last period and the three of us instantly clicked. I hung out with Lily and Andrea three or four times after school, and Andrea introduced King to Lily and me.

When I woke up, I originally intended on meeting up with Lily and Andrea before class. I was running a little late, so instead I headed straight to the cafeteria to grab breakfast instead of meeting with the girls.

"Kenzi! How are you?" I heard King yell to me. I was

confused seeing him, because during a conversation when we met, he mentioned to me he was going to a different school.

"I'm okay, I thought you went to Norwalk High?"

"I do, shhh," he replied, using exaggerated gestures as if he really was trying to hide his true identity. I couldn't help but laugh as I walked away. King was always up to something.

"Talking on the phone with Andrea a few days after seeing King, we decided to give him a call."

Coming back to the present, I began to tell Jodi about the last conversation I had with King before we got the news that he was no longer with us.

"He seemed so much better than he actually was, apparently. He sounded so regular, telling us about his girlfriend problems, how he was into church, and how much he was enjoying his new baby sister. In the school hallway was the last time I saw him before putting him to rest and that phone call was the last time we spoke. The story behind his death puzzles me.

"It is puzzling to me because for King to be such a happy person during the short time I have known him, I would not have thought taking his own life was on his agenda. Losing King was the first time I experienced the death of someone I knew. The passing of my family members happened later in life.

"The day I found out, I met with Andrea, and we walked down to Kings house to meet a few people from school. His family was not home at the time, so we sat on his porch and cried for hours. It was some type of comfort, you know? He used to sit out front all the time, so it felt like he was with us. We sat out there and reminisced about everything, from when each of us first met him until the last day we spoke to him."

"How did he pass away?" Jodi asked.

"He shot himself." I looked away as Jodi began to write something in her notepad.

"I'm sorry for your loss," she responded, "At a young age, in a new state, I can only imagine how traumatizing it may have been to go through that."

I looked out the window and my thoughts went back into that place.

"After King passed, it seems like nothing got better. I lost my virginity the following year, and my then on and off again boyfriend Ethan and I basically went to war after that."

Ethan and I began dating a month after King passed, we were always on and off. Only the Lord himself really knows why, but I was still positive that we would be together literally until "death do us part." That is how infatuated I was with him, and it was a very scary thing to feel in such a short period of time. Andrea was probably the only person who understood how much love I had for Ethan. Anything he did, whether it was right or wrong I'm always on his side. Even if something hurts me mentally or physically I will be his lawyer until the end, it was always him and me forever.

During the first year of our on and off relationship, Ethan was also on and off with many other females. It took me a whole year, standing by watching him do what he wants for me to finally decide to do what I wanted to do. Ethan told me on a drunk night he lost his virginity to an upperclassmen. I was only 13 years old, I was hurt and was not thinking rationally. After finding out what he did, I kept Ethan in my life but I also kept some male friends around who were there when I needed them.

"I lost my virginity to one of my "male friends" Ronnie, I explained to Jodi. "I had a crush on both Ronnie and a guy named Anthony when I was in high school. Ethan despised them both. Ronnie lived around the corner from Lily, so I went to visit him quite often."

October 14th was different though. That day, Ronnie and I had something special planned. Going up the stairs to his apartment, I felt my legs get weak. The nervousness was settling in but yet I still felt confident about my decision. I knew for sure that Ethan hurt me and I wanted payback. It did not matter to me if it was the same day, the next week, the next month, or year. I was just determined to get him back, Eventually.

As I walked up the stairs, all I could think about how I felt when I heard Ethan lost his virginity to someone else. I walked into Ronnie's room and saw he was well prepared; he had condoms, sheets on the floor, and a stereo next to it all. He always played his music really loudly, so the volume was normal to his parents and brothers. Even with the loud music I still jumped when I heard his voice.

"Are you ready?"

Am I ready? Of course I am. Obviously, if I am here I would hope I was ready.

"Yes" I responded out loud.

I watched him put the condom on and as he kept kissing me, I began to take my pants and underwear off. He was nervous, I felt him trembling, or maybe that was me? I was already lying down when he got on top of me. It isn't as bad as I pictured, I thought. It doesn't hurt much. It is actually pretty boring, what the hell do people get out of this?

I began thinking about how this would affect my relationship with Ethan. We were supposed to be each other's first everything, what happened? Ronnie kissed me, which completely took me out of my deep thought.

"Does it hurt?" he asked but I didn't respond "Are you okay?"

I knew that was coming next due to my lack of response. I shook my head "yes," hoping that would satisfy him. My phone lit up, and I looked over and checked it. Lily was sending me a text message. My heart started beating fast. I grabbed my phone to read the text and she said that she and her mother were outside waiting for me. I couldn't believe we were taking this long. I had completely lost track of time.

"What's wrong?" he asked me, I'm guessing he read my facial expression, which I'm not surprised. I mean, we are having sex right now, and I stopped to read a text.

"Jan and Lily are outside, what if Jan knows? What if she tells my mother?" I was panicking at this point, I'm almost positive he was too. I got up, bottoms on said my goodbyes and damn near ran outside to get in Jan's car.

"Hey Jan" I said once I sat down inside of the car.

"Hey, how come you left Lily" she asked.
Oh damn! What do I say to that? She didn't come because Ronnie and I wanted to fuck?

"She hadn't finished her homework so me and Ronnie just listened to music, we didn't realize it was so late"

Great response, I thought to myself. That was smooth. She told me not to worry about it and went on to telling Lily about her day. I'm glad she left the conversation alone and didn't dig too much deeper. As soon as I got home, I called Ronnie.

"Hey, what's up?"

"Nothing, how are you feeling?" he asked.

I didn't think he wanted my real response to that.

"I'm okay. Did you tell your parents?"

Ronnie is what I call a daddy's boy, Every time he does something his father has to know.

"Not yet. Are you going to tell your mother?"

Of course not, she's going to ask me why did I decide to have sex with some random boy rather than the person I have been with. Does it make sense for me to tell her? No, I decided, I will take this to my grave.

"Nope, I don't think I plan on telling her anytime soon. I

thought I was supposed to bleed. I do not know if we did it right." I responded a little confused as I looked at my naked body in the mirror.

"I don't know, maybe I should ask my mother?"

"NO! That's okay, I'll figure it out."

That was the last thing I wanted him to do. Don't get me wrong, I did like Ronnie somewhat, but his relationship with his parents was too much. I love a guy who loves his mother, but my business is my business and no one else's. I guess he isn't just a "daddy's" boy, because they both need to know everything.

"What ended up happening with Ronnie?" Jodi asked.

"I'm actually pretty ashamed to say, I left him about a week later. After losing my virginity, I blamed the break up on him telling his parents. He became clingy, and the next morning all I could do was stare at myself in the mirror for a while. I don't know what I was looking for. Maybe I was looking to see if I looked different, or trying to figure out if it was worth it. Maybe he wasn't even clingy, maybe he wasn't too close to his parents. I think I was the problem."

"Maybe, you just weren't used to that type of guy." Jodi responded.

"Maybe." It wasn't worth it though, not even a little bit.

"Ronnie needed to happen, you didn't understand it back then but I am sure you do now. You grew from the situation and that is the most important part." Jodi explained. "Back then, it was your turning point, it began the cycle that you are here to complete."

Over and Over:

Jodi was absolutely right. I wasn't used to a nice guy like Ronnie because I got so used to Ethan.
I became numb after he came into my life. My sophomore year; well, I'll be honest, all four years of high school were based on breaking his heart into small little pieces. I was living proof that the saying 'hurt people, hurt people' is true. I was doing things that I knew were not right, things I would care about under normal circumstances. I didn't care who I hurt in the process as long as I affected him.

"So, you broke it off with Ronnie. After that life changing event, that affected the both of you. What was his response?" Jodi wrote in her notepad as she spoke. "What was his reaction?"
I would think most males would be happy a girl was not attached after losing their virginity to a guy, but not Ronnie.

"Yeah, he was upset enough to tell his father. His father actually ended up having a long talk with me, which ultimately made it worse. Ronnie seemed weak to me after that. Why would he go and tell his father that I was breaking up with him? Why was his father threatening to tell my mother? I asked him not to tell anyone what happened between us. Clearly, he did the opposite. It even went as far as his aunt telling Lily and her mom that I was "fast" and must've done that before. When in all actuality I was simply a teenage virgin who happened to have an emotional disconnect for her nephew. I'm sure there are more people like me out there. Somewhere." I responded to Jodi as I shrugged my shoulders and fixed myself on the seat.

I never understood why he told his parents so much. That just was not something I wanted to deal with. We lived in a small community so I hurt Ronnie, the family knows and talks about me and then it gets out. To avoid that, I ended up having to tell my mom before someone else did! Hamden is not even close to being as big as Brooklyn.

I know I should have stopped myself with Ronnie, but Ethan kept hurting me so I had to get him back. Again.

"When all was said and done with Ronnie, I told Ethan and it felt so good to rub it in his face. It was like a "aha" moment! I was so happy to be one step ahead of him." I continued. "He was mad, yelled at me a little but he came right back. Like always. He came back and then embarrassed me by sleeping with a girl in my class. She knew about us and rubbed it in my face every chance she could. But then, I met Angel. He was older and really quiet. Quiet people intrigue me for some reason. Andrew was really quiet to until he laughed." I giggled. "I thought Angel was very cute, like a little kid though. Adorable, I should say. I saw him and Ethan speak a few times but honestly, who didn't Ethan speak to? He was outgoing and friendly, he knew almost everyone.
I got to know him and slept with him pretty quickly, it was not worth it, and just like with Ronnie, I was bored.

"When did Ethan find out about you and Angel?" Jodi asked.

"Well, after the third interaction between Angel and I. I told him myself because the point of my actions was to force him to feel how I felt. So, I started to sleep with people he knew. People he didn't like, and people I didn't even like. I just needed him to feel it."

"McKenzie, you cannot keep drinking poison, and expecting other people to die from it. Ethan may have been upset by your actions, but you were hurting yourself the most, by doing things you knew you should not be doing." Jodi had a point but I had a different thought process at the time.

"Ethan just kept sleeping around, he kept hurting me

over and over. But, Angel seemed to have hurt him the most for some reason, and his reaction told me that." Jodi looked at my face, trying to read my expression.

"What did he say or better yet, what did he do?" she asked.

"In high school, there were plenty of house parties, I used to go to almost all of them. Sometimes I'd go alone and meet friends or sometimes my partner in crime Lily and I would go together. This particular night, I went alone because I was meeting Ethan's brother David there. I did not know Ethan was going to be there. We didn't have any issues at the time anyway, so I wasn't really concerned, you know?" Jodi nodded. I took a breath before continuing.

"Well, once I got there I seen David and we hung out until the end of the party. He noticed Ethan motion me to come with him, I don't listen to anyone when it comes to him, but looking back, at times I wish I had listened."

"Do not go with him." David kept repeating himself.

"Okay, dad. I hear you but, I want to go. Plus, if I don't he will be mad at me and I don't want that."

David didn't care about Ethan being mad, he never did. He walked off after a few minutes but not before advising me that I need to learn to listen more because he knows more. I brushed it off and kept walking. I did wonder why Ethan needed Angel to come with us, but I didn't say much, I knew he was up to something, but couldn't pinpoint what it was.

"So, Kenz, you know Angel, right?" He didn't even look at me, but I heard the bullshit in his voice like he was waiting for this moment.

"What's your point?" He laughed his stupid laugh.

"Didn't you fuck him?" I stopped walking with them and began walking back to the party. I hated having to tell David I told you so, but it was cool.

"No, come on I'm joking, you know I love you." I didn't

say anything, he always loved me when it was convenient for him. He walked up the stairs of an abandoned home.

"Okay, why am I here?" Angel walked off and it was just Ethan and me standing there. He walked up behind me and began to kiss me on my neck.

"How can I help you?" I asked. I couldn't hold my rudeness in, I knew he was going to ignore me, but I asked anyway. He stuck his hand down my pants and attempted to pull my pants down. He looked over the back porch we were on and called for Angel.

"Yo, you wanna join us, my guy?" My heart fell to my stomach. I couldn't believe him, I pushed him away from me, but he grabbed me and kissed me.

"Nah, I'm okay. That's not my thing." Angel replied. I heard him talking, but I also noticed finally that Ethan was drunk. I slapped him and ran down the stairs.

Ethan didn't come after me to apologize. He didn't even call me to see if I was okay after walking home alone that night.

"Both of you, continued to betray each other" Jodi said.

"Yes, very much so. We were just going in circles and of course that wasn't the end of it." I was so weak to forgive him over and over, and he came back to me over and over.

A few weeks into the summer, Brittany moved in with us after all the back and forth she was dealing with at home. When she moved in our disagreements increased. They were stupid but they were happening every single day. We needed to get out of the house for some fresh air.

"Lamar, just called. He's with Gary and Ethan. Let's go hang out with them."

"Okay, I'm down." That was Brittany's usual response when I wanted to do something, so I wasn't surprised.

"Ma, we are going to hang out with Lamar. We'll be back later, okay?"

Atelophobia Extended Version

"No later than 11pm," she responded as we ran out the door. We ended up at Lamar's house less than 15 minutes later.

"Kenz!" I heard him yelling behind me. We walked back to where he was and greeted him at the garage door he was standing in front of. As we walked in, Ethan was standing on the other side of the garage with Gary and some guy I have never seen before right by the door next to them. This guy was someone I'd never met before, so I kept my distance from him and made sure Brittany did too. I looked up and saw she was giggling and smiling with Gary. He always watched out for us so I knew she was okay.

Lamar turned off the garage lights but somehow Ethan found me. He had a way of making me feel right at home. He held me for a while until he decided to kiss me, and things, of course, got intense. As he gripped my ass, I trembled. I don't know how he always gets me excited so quick. I pulled away from him and went over to where Lamar was at.

"Can I have some, bro?" He was drinking E&J. I hated the aftertaste, but I loved the feeling of being drunk. Once he passed me the bottle, Brittany and I ended up keeping the bottle to ourselves. Brittany and I loved to dance, and we danced with Lamar and Gary until I walked back over to Ethan.

"Yo, Kenz! We have to go" Brittany was trying to get my attention. I heard her, but when Ethan was around, I didn't know anyone else.

"Kenz man, get off of me." I know he did not like when I was drunk, but I didn't like it when he was high on whatever.

"Why? Don't you love me?" I asked in a slurred voice.

"No, I don't" he replied.

"Yes you do!" I went off on a tangent "I love you too, Even when you're smoking or popping E! I don't say shit, Fuck you Ethan!!"

35

As I grabbed his shirt my cell phone and iPod fell out of my pocket. I bent to pick them up and I felt a hand on my head. Ethan walked away as I bent down so I knew it couldn't have been him. This person's heavy hand was forcing me back down. I kept trying to pick up my head back up but he was too strong. "Help!!" I began to yell but no one came. I yelled a little louder and he finally let go and quickly walked away. I searched the garage for Brittany and grabbed her arm.

"Let's go!"

"Sis, what's wrong?" Lamar sounded panicked. I didn't want to make this guy look bad. That is always my problem. I'm always worried about how other people will look. Even though I definitely should speak up, I never know how.

"Mommy said we had to be home a while ago." I knew he wasn't going to let us go that easily but he could tell by my eyes that I did not want to be bothered.

"I'll walk you halfway."

I didn't even bother looking for Ethan; I knew he wasn't going to walk up the hill with us. He never did anything that benefitted me. I walked toward Main Street and did not bother to look back. Once we said our goodbyes to Lamar, Brittany asked me if my mother would be mad. I didn't answer her.

"Yo cousin, Ethan looked mad. What was wrong with him?" She asked.

"I don't know. He doesn't like when I drink but I don't care what he likes. He's bipolar."

I felt rage inside of me as I responded. I really did feel played. How could he leave me next to some strange man in the dark like that? I started to remember the times that he hurt me, and I just wanted to cry. But, I didn't know how to cry any more. I know he made me an angry person but I don't remember when I began to allow him to affect my emotions so much. I continued to do things to myself, for a reaction out of him but why? Where is this going to leave me? I just hoped my mother was asleep. I couldn't take a confrontation. As we walked through the back door and into the kitchen, I heard my mother's voice.

"Didn't I tell you two to be home at 11:00?"

"Sorry Cousin," Brittany apologized quickly.

"Lamar walked us home! We are alive, right? Relax." I couldn't help my attitude; knowing her, she was looking for a fight out of me and I was prepared to give her one.

"I have to pee. Excuse me." I walked into the bathroom and closed the door. Of course, once I sat down, she opened the bathroom door.

"Why don't you listen?" she asked.

"What happened," my step-father Brian inquired as he walked over to the bathroom half asleep. He had no clue what was going on or what was about to happen. Well, shit, neither did I.

"Are you drunk?" He asked me, as if I was going to answer. My mother suddenly came closer to me as I got up from the toilet. She put her hand in my face as she yelled about how disobedient I was. My siblings and Brittany were at the bathroom door watching as my parents yelled at me.

"Get out of my face," I yelled. My face turned red and I felt like I was going to explode; but I was very calm at the same time.

"Who the fuck do you think you are?" She yelled at me. Brian tried to push his way between us, but it was too late. We had already began fighting.

Session Two:

"She called my grandmother. I could talk to my Nana about anything, but at the time I was not up for talking. I probably shouldn't have come in the house drunk, but she didn't have to get into my face." Jodi seemed to disagree.

"I think you should own some responsibility for this. You cannot be that mad at her for something you played a part in. Think about it. You were under 21, living with your mother, and coming into her house drunk. Why wouldn't she be mad? If she couldn't get through to you, of course she'd call someone she knew could talk to you."

I nodded my head in agreement with Jodi. I couldn't really say too much to that. She had me there.

"That is one thing I do regret, putting my hands on her. I didn't have to hit her back but I did, I wasn't in my right mind." I had to admit.

"I'm glad you said that because that was my next question. What made you think that was okay? But, you answered my question before I could ask. You mentioned Ethan being high and never doing anything that benefited you. From the way that you explain the relationship it does not sound like love. It sounds like an addiction."

"I guess it was an addiction for the both of us. I like to help people, I always have. His mother wasn't around and his dad was not the best example. So, I figured I could teach him to be loving and caring. I thought, I could give him what he lacked you ---" I tried to explain.

"That was not your place, especially at such a young age." Jodi interrupted. She looked at the clock and we both noticed it is almost time to go.

"Okay, it's almost one. We have to wrap this up. That was a very intense session. I want you to go home and do

Atelophobia Extended Version

something for me. On a piece of paper, jot down what emotions you feel when you are talking about what you have gone through. When we meet again tomorrow at 10am, we will discuss it."

Jodi and I both got up and shook hands. I gathered my stuff to leave after saying my goodbyes, and went to my car. I pulled up to the house and saw Andrew playing outside with the boys. Tahj and Steven are four years apart, but you couldn't tell because of how well they get along. I thought they wouldn't want to be around each other, but I was wrong. They were best friends. Steven thought the world of Tahj, and Tahj protected his little brother no matter what -- and no matter whom -- he is up against. Sometimes he got himself in trouble standing up to the wrong person.

As I walked by, they stopped what they were doing to greet me. I loved hearing Tahj's little voice. Steven couldn't speak yet, but his gestures were enough for me.

"Hey bae, how did it go?" Andrew said. He was the most supportive man I've ever met. He never knocked me down; I was always good enough for him just as I was.

"It was okay. She gave me a mini assignment so I am going to go lay down and work on this. I'll get dinner started in a few, and I'll call you when it's finished."

I couldn't even begin to think about the emotions I was feeling in that office. Getting undressed, I began to look in our mirror at myself, the same way I did October 14, 2006. I have changed so much throughout the years, and I do not know how I held some of that stuff in for so long.

I lay down and grab my notebook, and begin to jot down:
1. I feel relieved
2. I feel angry and hurt all over again
3. I feel rejuvenated

I could only think of these three feelings. I didn't feel too many happy feelings, just betrayal mainly. But angry sums it all up for me. Sometimes I still feel stupid when I think about it, but I'll keep that to myself. I just felt like I should have loved myself more. I got up to begin making my boys something to eat. It would be cheeseburgers and french fries that night, and chicken nuggets for Tahj and Steven. That would be a surprise for them, but I was feeling good now that I was at home. I just wanted a quick dinner with a movie tonight.

"Dinner is ready, guys" I yelled out the front door. Tahj came running into the kitchen, and Andrew came in with Steven in his arms, came in right behind him.

"This is for me, Mommy?" Tahj asked.

I smiled. "Yes baby, it's for you."

The excitement on his face was cute; I had stopped him from eating nuggets a long time ago so I knew he missed it.

"Oh! This is great! Thank you, Mommy!"

Andrew kissed me. "Thanks babe."

I leaned over and kissed Steven as he sat in his high chair and my boys began to eat.

"So, what movie would you like to watch tonight? Tahj it's your turn to pick." When he had something on his mind, it was so evident. He thought hard about his decisions.

"Um, how about Smurfs 2!"

Oh gosh, not that movie again. He always wanted to watch the same movie over and over again until he got tired of it. Then he would pick another one to watch repeatedly.

Apparently, this time he wasn't thinking as hard as I thought. As soon as dinner was over, Andrew popped the DVD in and we watched it in the living room until the boys fell asleep.

"Are you tired yet?" Andrew asked me. I wasn't even watching it really; I guess you could say the movie was watching me.

"I just have a lot on my mind. I'll lie down though." I

didn't even realize I had tuned the movie out. Andrew got up to put Steven in his room, then came back for Tahj. Once both babies were out of the living room, I went into our room to lay in bed and fell asleep instantly.

The next morning, I got myself ready and then went to wake the boys.

"Mommy?" Tahj was already awake. He has always been a very light sleeper. I wasn't surprised that he had heard me coming.

"Oh, good morning, Mommy. Steven is still sleeping." I kissed Tahj.

"Good Morning, Tahj! How do you know Steve is still asleep?" I smirked.

"um, because I went into his room." He laughed and continued to watch TV.

"By the time Pop wakes up make sure you have your teeth brushed okay? I'll be back later, love you." I attempted to walk out the door and he stopped me.

"Um, Mommy?" Tahj said with curiosity in his voice.

"Are you leaving?" I smirked before answering; he forgets he's my son and not my man.

"Yes, I'll be back." That wasn't a good enough answer

"Where are you going Mommy?" I walked over to his bed and kneeled down next to him

"I'm going to a meeting I will be back to spend the day with you, Pop and Vic, is that okay?" I asked him.

"Oh! That's okay Mommy" he responded. I kissed him on the forehead, checked on Steven, and headed for the kitchen. Before I was done making my coffee, Andrew was already standing behind me.

"Do you have another appointment today?" He asked while turning me around to face him.

"Yeah," I responded as he kissed me on my forehead.

"Are you sure you can handle that? Back-to-back sessions with all of those emotions?"

I couldn't disagree with him. It was a bit much, but coming home to my boys made that better. Plus, I am kind of used to taking on more than I can handle.

"Yeah, I'll be okay. I only paid for two sessions to see how I would handle it. I'm not sure I want or need it to go past today. I'm glad I chose a black woman though."

"Why did it matter?" he asked.

"I feel like we are a little less judgmental. So, while I was telling her all of my secrets I felt comfortable. I didn't feel like I had "dumb nigger" written on my forehead."

I laughed, and he shook his head before kissing me on my forehead again.

"I love you. I just don't want you to be stressed, but I trust your judgment and I'm glad you are comfortable." I nodded my head.

"Thank you, bae." I said my goodbyes and went out the door and into my car.

As I arrived at Jodi's office, it was just hitting 10am.

"Perfect timing," I said to myself. I walked in and waited for her secretary to greet me and call me in to meet with Jodi. I knocked on her office door and waited for a response but there was none.

"Shit!" I heard her yell. The door was cracked so I peeked in and noticed she was cleaning up a spill.

"Do you need any help?"

"No, I'm okay. You startled me that's all."

"Oh, I apologize." I smirked.

"It's okay, I am reading a new book. The Shining by Stephen King. I ended up finishing The Quickie last night and I have been hooked on this book since! I don't know what I was thinking." She began to laugh as threw out her paper towel.

"Well, Good Morning, McKenzie. How was your evening after we parted ways yesterday?" Jodi pulled a seat up, sat down and crossed her legs with her notepad on her lap.

"It was a nice night. I had a movie night with my boys. I was a little distracted, but for the most part, it was a nice night," I responded.

"Oh? Why were you distracted?" Jodi asked. I thought back to yesterday and tried to come up with a simple answer.

"Well, I suppose everything we were talking about ran through my mind again once we sat down to watch a movie my son had picked out. I still can't believe I didn't love myself enough to not let certain things be done that I could have avoided."

"I know this may sound a little cliché, but keep in mind, you were young. You were able to learn from those mistakes and move forward. Look at you now." Jodi said as she smiled at me.

I nodded in agreement as she continued.

"Well, lets start where we left off from yesterday. What ended you and Ethan for good? What put you two at the finish line?" I smirked.

"Well, he moved on, I found out he was engaged with a baby boy on the way. I still cared about him but; I knew it was the end. After everything we both did to each other, he randomly moved on, so I really didn't have a choice. It's crazy, when people ask me what happened, they know we went through a lot; I know they are expecting some crazy story for me to tell. We simply just moved on from each other."

Jodi was writing in her pad as I was speaking. Her facial expression didn't change, and I was dying to know what she was writing down.

"I've noticed something about you, McKenzie. It really does take a lot out of you for you to leave or try something new. Are you afraid of new situations, relationships, friendships, etc?" When Jodi asked me that, I thought she could read my mind or something, as if this therapy was a waste of time and she had secretly known me my whole life.

"Yes, I'm petrified. So I'd rather try to keep you around no matter what our situation is just to have an excuse not to meet someone new."

"Why?" she asked, and I looked away.

"I never thought someone would love me as much as he did." It was probably a stupid response to her, but that's truly how I felt.

"Well, how can someone love you, if you don't love yourself? In order to love yourself, you have to remind yourself you are good enough for better. You cannot allow bad things to happen to you, and do bad things with your body to hurt other people. When someone loves themselves it shows and from the way you present yourself I can tell you learned how to, but I can also tell when you were younger you didn't know how." I looked away again.

"You're right. I should have left him after the first incident. It didn't stop with him either, with the absence of Ethan I was attached to someone else. I wasn't in love with him at all, I actually used him to make someone else mad, but our relationship was toxic; physically and mentally abusive. I probably should have listened to my friend and left it alone." Jodi took her glasses off and sat back.

"So, who is he?"

Growing Pains:

As I noticed Jodi get comfortable, I looked back out the window and tried to explain this complicated situation. I thought back to the year after I graduated from Hamden High.

"I really do not like Jake. He is trying too hard." I remember telling my friend Lauren.

Lauren and I met during Junior year in high school and we kept in touch after graduation. We were close from the beginning. She was loud, honest and outspoken. I know I could expect some honesty from her.

"So, why don't you tell him you aren't interested?"

Lauren was right. I shouldn't have even bothered with him but at the same time, I was bored.

"I think I'm going to do it, Lauren; just play with him for a short while," I told her as I started to giggle.

"What, bitch? Are you confused? Don't play with that boy." She's right but, I don't care.

"I had no intentions of being serious with him. It was just for my amusement. I should have listened to her because it wasn't fair to him."

"Do you regret playing with him?" Jodi asked, cutting into my memory of that conversation. I took a moment before answering. I had to really think about that one.

"Playing with his heart, yes. I definitely regret that because no one deserves it. But without any of those mistakes, I don't think I would have been where I am today. We were fine for a while though, until he found out about the cheating. It doesn't justify what he did, but I understand his anger somewhat."

"Well, how did he find out?" Jodi's question made me

feel bad, simply because I know I did everything wrong in the situation.

"Every time I would get mad, I would remind Jake who I really wanted to be with. I also always had one male friends around. I never ended friendships with any of them. He kept a lot from me too though. It took me getting pregnant for the first time to find out about Kelly."

Jodi's face changed, "Who's Kelly?" Jodi jotted down something in her notepad and looked up at me so that I could begin again.

"Kelly is a girl he was talking to before me. I knew of her, but like most guys he said she was crazy, and it was barely a friendship. Maybe I was the crazy one for believing him."

"Clearly, he was lying, right?" Jodi asked.

"Yeah, I found out after my abortion that he actually never stopped talking to her." I bet she was probably wondering where the fighting came in; I heard when a guy is angry with you for no reason it's usually because the other girl made him mad. Now, looking back I wouldn't doubt that was the case most of the time.

"A few months into the relationship, I was young and careless. After he said he loved me it went down hill from there. I began to lie and say it back while still having friendships with other guys. I didn't sleep with anyone else, but I just wasn't into him the way he needed me to be. I eventually learned when you string someone along, it is enough to drive them crazy. The person can become obsessed, or really angry, and it isn't a good look after that. He wasn't okay with me being friends with males. He was very possessive. I had more male friends than female friends, and he couldn't understand that I was always this way, and I still am."

Jodi took a sip of water and adjusted her glasses before she said, "go on." I took another breath.

"The first time he hit me, I did not understand. I mean,

when I got mad I said bad things, and I own that, but I do not understand why he'd get mad about every person who came in contact with me."

I thought back to the first time we had an altercation at Jakes mother's house. Waking up somewhere I knew I wasn't supposed to be was scary, but knowing your "boyfriend" could flip on you at the drop of a dime was a much scarier feeling.

I woke up and Jake was not in the room. What should I do? I really had to use the bathroom, but I didn't want his mother to see me. I guessed I would just wait for him, which really was my only option at that point. Jake walked into the room and I knew there was something on his mind. I had just had my abortion two weeks ago, I was still stressing about my own issues. I really didn't have the energy to argue with anyone.

"Were you fucking with Jordan?" he interrupted me in mid thought with bullshit I was not up for.

"Are you serious?" He had to be crazy, right? What the hell, he must have been.

"Yes, I'm serious! You're a fucking hoe! First Damien, then Jordan? Aren't they best friends? Jordan is my cousin. How could you betray me and make me look dumb? You know I hate looking dumb." I looked at the clock and noticed the time as he went on with his rant. It's too early for this.

"Think what you want. I don't give a fuck. Jordan is my best friend, I would never go out with him, and if I am such a hoe, leave me the fuck alone then." I got off the bed as Jake's mom walked into the room. Jake began to throw his clothes, sneakers and television everywhere. Anything he could get his hands on flew across the room. He always went from zero to a thousand within seconds.

"Jake! Stop it" she yelled.

"No! Leave McKenzie, get the fuck out," he yelled at me. I was already getting dressed but he was trying to keep my things from me. I was confused; I just really wanted to get home.

"Jake, just leave me alone. Excuse me, Ms. Walker. I will walk home."

"Can you call someone to pick you up?" she asked.

"I'll walk," I replied as I tried to walk past her. Her son was still on his rampage, literally destroying everything in his way. Somehow, I did not think he would be coming for me next. He slapped me on the side of my face. All I could do was turn around and stare.

"I was stuck, I didn't react," I told Jodi next. "I just looked up at Jake while his mother screamed and yelled for him to go out the room and out of her house."

"You are just like your father! Not in my got damn house! Get out now!" Mrs. Walker yelled. With all of these emotions churning inside of me, I could not make any sense of what had just happened.

"Come on baby," Mrs. Walker said soothingly. "I'll take you home."

I walked downstairs and went straight to her car.

"What was going through your mind after you walked out of the room with his mother?" Jodi asked, bringing my thoughts back to the present and I smirked.

"I am anti abortion, and was very angry that I got one, but I just kept replaying over and over in my head thank God I didn't keep it."

"Are you okay?" Ms. Walker asked

Do I look okay bitch?, what type of question was that?

"No, I'm not, but I will be," I answered respectfully.

"What happened?" she asked.

"I'm not really sure. He said someone told him I have been cheating, which isn't true. I just had an abortion."
I figured out he didn't tell her by the look on her face. He wanted me to keep a baby his mother did not know about? Oh great, I thought. This is epic.

"Abortion? When was this? How far were you? Did your mom know?" His mother bombarded me with questions.

"Two weeks ago. He told me you wouldn't like me because of the abortion. Maybe that's why he didn't tell you."

We arrived at my house, and I knew I couldn't go inside. My lip was bleeding, and I could not think of an excuse to come up with to explain it, since I was supposed to be at my friend Jasmine's house. I said goodbye to Ms. Walker and walked to my backyard. I called Jasmine to fill her in on what happened at Jake's house. I walked down the avenue. I was almost at the next street when I remembered I had on pajamas, and I had to go home. I walked back down the avenue and through the back door, but of course my mom was near the back door, in the kitchen. Cooking and cleaning was an every day thing for her so I was far from surprised to find her there.

"Hey, Puddin! Had fun?" She didn't notice my lip. Maybe it wasn't so bad?

"Yeah I had fun," I responded as I walked past her, headed to the bathroom. "Jasmine's little sister Natasha is getting so big. Kids grow fast." I walked into the bathroom to look in the mirror. It was bad, but not as bad as I thought. I still can't figure out why he would believe such a lie when I am still recovering from the abortion. My mom had her back toward me when I walked back into the kitchen to go upstairs so she did not see my face. But I knew I had to come up with something quick; there was no way I could hide this for long.

"Did she eventually see your lip?" Jodi's question brought my focus back to our session.

"Yes, she did. I told her I was rough housing. Being a tom boy paid off."

"Did the fighting stop there?" Jodi asked.

"As bad as this may sound, no it did not stop there.

Looking back, I realize now that if he can put his hands on me in front of his mother, I should have left him alone. Parts of me wish I had walked away at that very second, but you live and you learn."

All I kept thinking about as I sat there was how his mother had not reacted the way I thought she should. It was as if it was normal for men to put their hands on a female. Because I was expecting a reaction from her, I had failed to react.

From time to time even now, I think back and ask myself "What if I...?" But then I snap back to reality. No matter what I had done or had not done, I could not have changed Jake. You cannot help a person who does not want to be helped. I noticed Jodi staring at me, trying to read my expression I suppose.

"What is on your mind, McKenzie?" Jodi inquired.

"I'm just realizing it wasn't my fault the way Jake mistreated me. I can't blame myself for this. I couldn't control the situation. Now that I look back, we both treated each other badly, but there was no reason for him to put hands on me. I wasn't actually cheating with the people he kept accusing me of cheating with. I don't understand why he'd hit me for something that he was completely wrong about. With Jake, it was always fight first, ask questions later, and it bothered me that I could not control it. I could not stop him from what he was doing to me, hurting me for no real reason. I ended up wanting to control everyone and everything else around me to avoid ever being hurt again."

I explained to Jodi how weak and vulnerable I always felt. I was afraid of him, but I honestly felt like Jake was the only one who loved me at that time. My family and I were just starting to mend things after I acted out in High School, they were slow at forgiving. I no longer had Ethan to distract me, he was the only person who took the time out to get to know me.

"The fighting became scary; after he slapped me that first time, at his mother's house, it seemed to open doors for him to abuse me, not only physically but mentally as well. He knew I longed for acceptance. He knew I thought he accepted me."

"A lot of women seek acceptance from men when they don't have a father or father figure. But you had Brian. So, tell me about your biological father," Jodi Insisted.

"Well, my father went to jail when I was a few days old, but my mother met Brian and he raised me from the time I turned one. That is all." Jodi took off her glasses and this time she sat up and looked into my eyes.

"Usually, when people behave a certain way, you know, entertain people who do bad things to them, and allow people to stay in their lives who don't deserve to be there. It is because they are looking for love. When you need someone to love you, it doesn't matter where the love comes from, even if it isn't real love. You still need to feel that someone cares."

I looked up at Jodi. I thought I knew where she was going with this.

"So, McKenzie, do you have a relationship with your biological father?" I shook my head.

"No, I don't and I don't want one."

"See, you say that, but I don't believe you. You told me yourself you want acceptance. I don't think you spent all your time in high school just upsetting Ethan. You were looking for male attention to fill that void left by your father. Does your real father have any other kids?"

I looked out the window and then back at Jodi "Yes, two younger than me and one older."

She looked into my eyes again.

"Does he have a relationship with them?" I nodded my head "yes," as tears started to well up in my eyes.

"I don't understand why he always took care of them

and not me. What made them so special? Why was that upperclassmen good enough for Ethan to give his virginity to? Why couldn't he wait for me? Why couldn't I be his only one? Why is it that my family is so biased?" I couldn't help it; I broke down.

"You know, Tahj had to be about one and a half years old. By then, me and his father split. I was testing the waters, literally just having fun. There was this guy named Lex. He was a rapper, I slept with him because he was cute. I told his friend who was dating Mariah at the time, that I wanted him sexually. So, he made it happen. Lex became my on and off sex partner for about two-three years but during our off time I met this guy. Kevin. He was an older Jamaican man who I met in a club. I was not trying to sleep with him though, I just thought he may be cool to hang out with." Jodi handed me a tissue and I continued.

"He picked me up one day, he asked me to go to his house to watch a movie. But, when we got there he didn't just want to watch a movie. He began to take advantage of me. I cried, screamed and kicked him off of me until he finally stopped and decided to bring me home. At that point, I just knew I wasn't worth shit. Excuse my language, but it was like ... I could not find the value in myself, the people around me did not see it and even strangers, people who barely knew me just knew I didn't matter and they can get away with anything." I explained in between sniffles.

"McKenzie, you can't blame yourself for the way other people are. You have to be okay with the idea of never knowing why people do the things they do. Ultimately it's their loss, you have to remind yourself that you are perfectly fine, and the people who deserve you have you in their lives." Jodi handed me tissue and kept talking.

"Do you mind if I ask you another question about him?"

"No, I don't mind," I responded.

Atelophobia Extended Version

"How is your biological father's relationship with your mother?" I thought back and looked away again.

"Horrible. When I was growing up, all he ever did was talk bad about her. Nothing good ever came out of his mouth. I hated him for it, but I pretended to like him because he is my father. My mother and Brian did everything for me and they still do. All he did was disappoint me and he still does that too." I noticed Jodi writing in her notepad. For some reason, I went back thinking about my biggest fight with Jake.

"I remember when Brian was away on a business trip and I came home with a black eye one night. I blamed it on Lamar and I wrestling. I told my mom that Lamar had elbowed me, and she acted like she believed it.

"When I went in my room to lie down, I wished I could call my real father the way his son was able to call him for anything, the way girls could call their dads for help, since Brian, my other dad, was away. I was so angry I began to believe the negative things my birth father would say about my mother driving him away. I was angry with her for years, until I opened my eyes."

"What made you open your eyes?" Jodi asked me.

"I began to try and impress him. I became a Realtor and an Investor the same year I found out I was expecting Tahj. I wanted to show him I was independent and could make my own money. I made sure I went to college right after Real Estate School was over, juggling School, an infant and showing homes is a lot to take on at once. Nothing I was doing mattered to him though, he barely acknowledged it. I never even heard him say he was proud of me.

"During the middle of my pregnancy with Steven, I prayed a lot about my relationships with Brian, Andrew, my mom, and my biological father to be specific. I decided to forgive my father for the way he talked about my mother, and the way he did not acknowledge me so that I could move forward with my life. I did want to try one more time to allow him to be in his grandson's life as well as mine.

"I texted him saying hello and received no response for him, but my step-mom called me and told me he told her I texted him! I instantly became annoyed, so I texted him again. Maybe I shouldn't have, but I did. I told him why I had reached out to him, and how it had hurt my feelings that he hadn't bothered to respond.

We went back and forth once he responded. He told me I was disrespectful, so he stopped speaking to me. It wasn't an argument at first; I was just confused because I hadn't spoken to him in a year. So I didn't understand how I could have been disrespecting him." As I shared these memories with Jodi, the look on her face told me she was just as confused about that as I was.

"Well, did he explain what he was referring to?" Jodi finally asked.

"Actually, now that I think about it," I answered, "he never did respond to that specific question but he went on to talk about other things."

"You're just like your mother you hear?" He texted back. I know my mother does not talk to this man so if she's being disrespectful too I know he's delusional.

"What are you talking about?" I texted back.

"Your attitude is just like hers and I can't stand it!" he replied. I came back from my memory and looked at Jodi.

"Oh, okay," I said to her. "So inviting this man to my baby shower is giving him attitude and reminding him of my mother? That was interesting."

I stopped for a moment to catch my breath before telling Jodi about the rest of the text exchange.

"I'm a little tired of you talking about my mother every chance you get," I wrote back. "Keep her out of this. I texted you to invite you to my baby shower, not to argue about her or anything else actually."

I felt myself about to explode responding to him in the politest way I knew how. I could not and would not tolerate anyone talking about my mother, especially now that I was old enough to tell him what was really on my mind.

"Are you bi-polar?" He responded. "You need to get some pills and stop making stupid decisions, having these damn kids! What is wrong with you?"

I stopped thinking about those text messages and began to talk directly to Jodi.

"Jodi, I lost it after reading that text. I can hear someone talk about me all day long, but when they talk about certain people, especially my kids and my mother, we're going to war."

"I don't blame you," Jodi responded as she shook her head.

"I'm sorry you had to deal with that from him McKenzie, and it's weird because the memory you are recalling is confusing. He still never explained why he doesn't speak to you. The only thing I got from his last text message was that you reminded him of your mother. Whatever he has against your mother, and whatever she did or did not do, it seems like he's holding it against you."

I nodded my head at Jodi, saying "Too bad it took me years to figure all of that out. I told him that I realized he doesn't like me," I continued, "because he can't have her and that's not my fault or my kids' fault. I reminded him how he had co-signed for me to get an apartment so that he could stop paying child support earlier than he would have otherwise. He was supposed to pay for my medical insurance and for college, but he got out of all of that once he had the child support cut short. I realized he wasn't the man for any of us, and he never would be." Jodi smirked.

"He definitely isn't the one for you or your mother, and especially not your little boys. But you have to admit Brian is amazing for filling his shoes. I'd be lying if I told you that getting past what your father has done and how he has made you feel will be easy.

"What I will tell you is that you have to forgive yourself for believing in him and thinking highly of someone who didn't deserve it. Forgive yourself for being mad at your mother. Forgive yourself for thinking Ethan was worth your time. Forgive yourself for thinking you were doing something wrong by trying to get along with your cousin. Forgive Jake, and let it go. Remember, Forgiveness isn't for the other person it is for you. Being spiteful, bitter and overcompensating is not healthy for you."

I smiled at her as she got up to get two bottles of water.

"Thank you," I said as she handed me one. "Brian is and will always be my dad. It's not his fault that I went through these things, he never made me feel like I wasn't good enough."

"So, Andrew? What is the story with him?" Jodi inquired with a smile.

New Beginnings:

Every girl wants that perfect love story right? You know, falling in love, getting engaged, marriage, moving in together with her dream husband. Beginning a family in your new home with the white picket fence. Am I close? Most females want to fall in love with their first love, stay in love, and live the perfect life. I know I did. I really did think Ethan was going to be my first and last love. I thought we were going to end up going to college, that he was going to get drafted into the NBA, and we would live happily ever after.

You could tell it was just young love though. Don't get me wrong; sometimes this dream does work out. But, now-a-days not so much because it seems almost impossible because people no longer want to work hard and stay committed to a relationship. I always had faith in eventually having something real. Andrew gave me something real.

"Well, his name is Andrew Austin," I told Jodi. "We met when I moved to Connecticut. I did "date" him when we were young, but it didn't last long. He was too good of a guy for me to hurt or play games with so, I left him early on. He remained a good friend. He would walk me home after school, and I'd go play basketball at his house. This was before we dated, and after.

"He never changed. My mom loved him, and so did my siblings. He was just an all-around nice guy. I remember in high school he was in a relationship with the same girl most of the time. I was a little jealous, I can honestly admit that.

"I kept having conversations with Andrea about what might happen if things worked out between Andrew and me. Even though we were young, I still had the "what if" question in my head. I even prayed about it. I asked God why

Andrew kept coming into my head. Why couldn't I stop thinking about having a life with him? Looking back, I know I was manifesting what we have today. I put so much energy into wanting him and it happened.

"I don't like the feeling of being jealous, but I respected his little situation at the time. Kind of. Sometimes, I'd go out of my way to hug him a little tighter and longer if she was looking. Tell him I missed him and loved him before walking away when she was standing next to him. BUT, as far as physical contact passed a hug I kept my distance. His girlfriends attitude was disgusting and she reminded me of Jake, possessive.

"After high school, he and his girlfriend broke up, and he reached out to me shortly after on Facebook because I put up a sad status. He was checking on me to see how I was doing. He was always the type to care even when he didn't need to. He had a big heart. Once we began talking again, we instantly got back to where we had left off.

"He became something like a best friend again -- when he wasn't giving me a headache of course. He always accepted me in any shape or form: as a tomboy, a mommy, and so on. I finally let him meet Tahj when he turned two years old and they clicked instantly."

I looked at Jodi, and I couldn't stop smiling, thinking back to the beginning of my life with Andrew.

"You must really love him. You haven't stopped smiling since I mentioned his name." Jodi smiled at me, "So, obviously he is Steven's father right?"

"Yes, even thought it was bittersweet for us to find out about Steven. I wasn't ready nor expecting to have another child, and neither was he. But we talked about it and prepared for the baby's arrival. It was his first kid, he was nervous and it was tough because we weren't in the best situation, but we stuck it out. Half way through my pregnancy even with the drama he asked me to marry him."

I thought back to January of that year.

"Kenz, are we still going shopping for the baby shower today? We're all going to meet at my sister's house right?" Andrew asked.

"Yes, we are. I just sent my mother a text so she can meet us at Danielle's." I yelled back to him from the bathroom.

It always took me longer to get ready than Tahj and him. I had make up and hair to do. I hoped he wasn't being sarcastic with that "are we still going" stuff. Andrew is good for being sarcastic with me.

After 20 minutes, I was finally ready. We got into the car and headed to Danielle's house. Everyone was already there just waiting for us. I was getting ready to walk into the house when I noticed everyone was gathering near the front door.

"Should I go back in the car? Are we leaving right this minute?" I was a little confused. They were all staring at me and then my mother stepped out from the group.

"Yes, we're getting ready to leave, Puddin. I just wanted to speak to Drew and Tahj before we got into our cars."

I noticed Tahj running over to me with a little box in his hand.

"Here you go Mommy, I love you," He said as we hugged each other tightly.

I opened the box and was surprised to see nice stud earrings, which I absolutely love. As I reached down to kiss Tahj, I noticed Andrew kneeling down behind him. Andrew also had a little box in his hand, as he opened the box up all I could hear were expressions of "aw" and "oh my gosh" coming from behind me.

"Will you marry me?" Andrew asked. I began to cry and I couldn't say a word.

I smiled at Jodi now.

"I said yes," I said as I flashed my ring at her. "Once Andrew came back into my life, he made me comfortable.

He was one person I did not have to be absolutely perfect for. I can wake up cranky, hair messed up, teeth not brushed, and he'll still tell me how beautiful I am. He made me realize imperfection is beauty. Still, because of all the bad things I had gone through, and how much I didn't love myself, I tried to be perfect in every other way. I had worked hard to accomplish things the same year I had Tahj. My father may not have noticed my accomplishments, so I used them as a confidence booster. Andrew didn't care about any of the money I had made he just cared about me. My accomplishments to Andrew were just a plus. He was proud to have me, he accepted me flaws and all.

"Wow, McKenzie," Jodi said, smiling. "I'm really proud of you. I literally met you yesterday, and you've already come to the realization that you are worth more than you gave yourself credit for when you were younger. You just needed someone you felt comfortable talking to. I did notice you have only scheduled two sessions with me. Were you trying to see if this was the type of help you needed?" I nodded.

"I did tell Drew I paid for two sessions to see if I would want or need anymore sessions but I'll be back after the honeymoon." I assured her. "Releasing these feelings and admitting my role in the situations was the first step for me. Now, I have to take a step back into reality, live my new life, and enjoy it. But I may need some help. My mind tends to wander back into the past and I can't mess my future up."

"Well," Jodi smiled, "I'm here when you need me. You have my number. Just schedule an appointment and I'm here to talk and listen."
She smiled my way and took a breath.

"So, when Is the wedding?" I felt my face light up all over again.

"August 13th[h]," I said, bursting into a bright smile.

"OH! In TWO weeks? Are you ready? Oh my! That is so exciting!" Jodi yelled while taking a peek at her calendar.

"I'll bring photos and tell you all about it!" I smiled at Jodi as I stood up.

"McKenzie, you never went into details about Tahj, you said you were 19 when you had him and that was it. But, I guess we can save that for next time." Jodi smiled as she hugged me "Good luck McKenzie! See you soon!"

I hugged Jodi and left her office. As I headed to my car, I noticed how beautiful it was outside. I pulled my compact mirror from my purse, smiled at my reflection, and put my shades on before I got into the car.

There may still be some unresolved feelings that I have yet to discuss but for now, the challenge is keeping the negativity from the past out of my future. Two weeks went by quickly since my last visit with Jodi. The wedding was beautiful and I would hate to allow my insecurities to get in the way of the new union we just created.

"Good Morning Babe!" I heard from Andrew.
"Good Morning!" I yelled back.
I got out of bed and headed into the bathroom with him. Before I entered I stood at the door and admired him. I finally married my best friend, who knew? I hugged Andrew from behind before reaching past him for my tooth brush.

"Are you ready to get back home?" He asked.
"Yes, I am! I miss the boys, and it's time for me to go see Jodi again." I replied.

Andrew put his toothbrush away and stepped back to look at me.

"I thought you wouldn't be continuing those sessions with her." I really do not know why he mentioned that, when he knew I had a great experience with her.

"I'm sorry dad, is that okay with you?" I laughed. "I told you that I was only going to see how it went and it ended up going better than I imagined. So, I'd like to continue because those two sessions weren't enough for me."

I kissed him on the cheek after putting my toothbrush away.

"Okay, I'm just not sure how I feel about you bringing up old memories and reliving those situations. I told you that before but it's okay, I have faith in you." Andrew replied as he followed me back into the hotel bedroom.

"Let's go get breakfast." I said back to Drew.

He got dressed faster than me for once. I'm on vacation mode until tomorrow, No rushing for me! I went over to the drawers looking for my sun dress. As I put on my dress I noticed Andrew watching me.

"Yes?" I asked.

"Nothing, I just feel lucky." He responded with a smirk.

I grabbed my shades and my wristlet and headed out the door towards the elevator.

It is beautiful out here in Honolulu. 85 degrees at 8:30am? I can get used to warm weather all the time. The Trump International Hotel's breakfast buffet called "In-Yo Café" has a great selection so we decided to stay at the hotel for Breakfast instead of leaving.

"Good Morning" the greeter said to us as we walked in.

"Good Morning" we both replied. We scanned the room, looking for a table.

"Found One!" I said as I walked over to the empty table I wanted to sit at.

"You go first and I'll watch your bag babe." Andrew suggested.

"Okay." I said as I walked away. I grabbed a plate and looked over my options. Pancakes, Bacon, Sausage, OH! They have Turkey Bacon and Turkey Sausage, Awesome!

I chose what I wanted to eat and I could not help but think about Joshua and how I could not wait to tell Jodi about our conversation. It took place right before the wedding. I am shocked at how I reacted when I seen him, I was not ready. My heart did not skip a beat or anything and I am definitely not missing him but I can't lie and say I was not mad as hell. How dare he tell me I was not big small enough but his girlf -----

"Honey, are you okay?" Andrew said as I approached our table. Apparently I had an attitude written on my face.

"Yeah, just thinking." I replied and sat down in my chair.

"Okay, I'll be back." Andrew went and grabbed his food rather quickly.

We sat, ate, talked and enjoyed each others company. After we were done we got up, headed upstairs and finished packing.

"Maybe we can go to the beach and just hang out" Drew proposed after our packing was done.

"Okay, lets go, let me just change really quickly." I went into the bathroom with my bathing suit and noticed Drews' phone was charging in the bathroom. As I was going to yell to him the phone lit up with a text that came through saying:

"I can't wait to see you!"

Who in the hell? I thought to myself. This cannot be happening on my honeymoon. Maybe it is a family member? Or a co-worker? But why would ...

"Bae?" he interrupted my thoughts. "Are you ready or?"

"Yeah, I'm coming." I replied back. Okay, I'll have to worry about this later when we are home. I finished up in the bathroom and ended up out of the hotel room for him. We got down to the beach and laid our towels out. Andrew laid on his back and I got on top of him.

He laughed, "I can never lay on my back without you finding your way on top of me."

I smirked at him. "Yes, this is true."

I laid down placing my head on his chest. My favorite sound is his heart beat, my favorite pillow is his chest. Even if it is a hard pillow! I hope he isn't talking to anyone he should not be talking to. Especially finding out on our honeymoon, oh man.

"Babe, let's go get in the water for a few." Andrew said interrupting my thoughts as always.

I got up and stretched, he got up as well and we headed to the water.

"Andrew! You know I can't swim!" I yelled as he tried to go off without me. He turned around and smiled.

"Yes, I know but how will you learn how to swim on your own if you are on my back all the time?" I ignored his question and latched onto his back.

"Who cares, let's go!" I laughed as he shook his head and began to guide me through the water.

He went under water and took me with him without warning. After that we began to play, splashing each other with water, hugging and kissing. We laughed and played and laughed some more for an hour or so.

"Come on, let's go upstairs. I'm getting tired." I yawned talking to Drew.

"It's only around 2pm, we just had breakfast a few hours ago and now you're ready for bed?" Andrew loved the outside, I loved the inside. This has been and probably always will be an ongoing struggle.

"Okay, you stay and I'll go." I responded as I headed towards shore.

I grabbed my towel and heard Andrew behind me, I smiled. Even with all the shit he talks, he's never too far behind. We headed back upstairs and we hoped in the shower together.

I got out first and got straight into the bed. Andrew is right, I am more tired than usual but I was so stressed about the wedding planning I think that since it is over I just need some rest. Andrew got in the bed and I found my head on his chest. He ran his fingers through my hair and I felt my eyes getting heavy.

"When I wake up, we will go back out I promise." I whispered to Drew.

He kissed me on my forehead and pulled me closer. "I love you" he whispered back, "get some rest."

I woke up and looked at the clock. It is 6pm, three hours passed! Oh no. Andrew isn't in bed, where is he?

"Bae?" I yelled, "Drew!"

I grabbed my robe and got out of bed to check the bathroom. Bathroom is empty, his phone is gone. I picked up my phone and proceeded to send him a message on WhatsApp:

"I am awake, Where did you run off to?"

I sat and stared at my phone waiting for a response. Did he text that number back while I was asleep?

"Oh, you're awake Finally! I got hungry and came down for food. I will be up in a minute"

He is always hungry, no surprise there. But did he text her back though? The number was not saved and I can only remember a few of them. It was definitely a 203 number, and then 414-2...what were those last three digits? Think Kenz! Damn! Well, what can I do from Hawaii anyway? I should just wait like I originally decided.

I laid back and placed my head on the pillow. But did he text her back though?

"Kenz!" Andrew said as he entered back into the room.

"Yeah?"

"Oh, what's wrong?" He asked.

"I am just ready to go home" I responded as I leaned over and picked up the room service menu from the night stand. "I am ordering room service since you already ate while I was asleep."

"Hello, Room 562? What can I get you?" The server answered.

"Hello, I'd like to order the Filet Mignon with a Baked Potato on the side. Is it alright if I have broccoli as my vegetable?"

"Sure not a problem, anything else?" The server asked.

"Oh, yes! A brownie sundae" I added while shooting a look at Drew. The hotel was booked with his debit card on file. He rolled his eyes my way and kept eating his meal.

"Okay I will be up in about twenty minutes." She replied

"Okay, Great!" I replied with a smirk. If she is here in twenty minutes I will give her a generous tip too!

"Are you upset that I left to go eat?" Andrew asked.

"No, I am just ready to go home."

"So, you bought that expensive ass meal because you're ready to go home?" He looked both annoyed and confused.

"Shut - UP" I replied as I laid back down

Did he text her back though? Ugh! Oh man, I can't wait to see Jodi.
After twenty minutes with the pillow over my face the knock came at the door but Andrew got to it first.

"I hope you gave her a nice tip." I said to him while taking my plate out of his hands.

"Be - Quiet" he responded. I smirked and walked over to the bed.

I quietly enjoyed my food as Drew flicked through the channels.

"Come to Bed" I said to him once I was finished eating.

"Well, it is only 7:42, you know I don't like to just lay in bed."

"What?" I responded with an attitude.

"You're so damn spoiled" he replied as he got into bed. He stopped turning the channel. "Oh, Teenage Mutant Ninja Turtles - Out of The Shadows."

"Yes!!!!" I said sitting up. "Omg, where is bad ass Ralph?? He has some whooping to do"

"Well, that woke you up" Andrew said. He got up from

the sofa he was eating on and came to lay down. He turned his back to me as if my excitement just created a problem.

"Goodnight Andrew" I said with a smile.

"Goodnight McKenzie"

Dumb-Stupid-Retarted:

"Good Morning, bags are packed! Let's go!!" I yelled with excitement.

"How long have you been up?" Drew asked as he sat up and stretched his arms.

"I've only been up since 5am."

"Only?" he asked with a confused expression."

"Well, the flight is at 8:45 it's 6:30 now. We have to eat, get to the airport, check our luggage, use the bath-- "

"I get it, I am up give me a few minutes." He stood up and proceeded into the bathroom. I slipped my sandals on and grabbed my phone to send a text.

"Hey Mom! We are leaving soon, I know the boys can't wait until they see their favorite parent, also known as me! Mommy!"

"What are you smiling about?" Andrew walked in as I was putting my phone down.

"Oh Nothing" I laughed and hopped up to give him a hug "I'm just in a good mood."

My phone lit up with a WhatsApp message from mommy:

"That's funny, because all they have been asking for is Andrew. See you soon!"

Figures.

Our travel time from the hotel to the airport was faster than coming from the airport. No traffic and a quicker check in process. I guess it is easier to send us back home instead versus welcoming us in.

"Once we land I am going straight to bed." said to Andrew as we fastened our seat belts on the airplane.

"Why don't you take a nap now? So that we can spend time with Steven and Tahj later?" He asked.

I smiled "Okay, you're right. Let's pray that I get enough rest."

"The flight is ten hours, why wouldn't you get enough rest? You should get more than enough really. Who actually sleeps for a full 8 hours anyway?" At this point, it seems like he is thinking out loud.

"Well, I was up waiting for you since 5am. So, hush and enjoy your view." I responded while giving him a sharp look.

Everything is not debatable. I shut my eyes and my mind began to wonder. He's so focused on me and my sleep. He really needs to focus on that missed text. For his sake it better not be Ms. "I can't let go because he really loves me even though he married you ass" Tammy!

"Bae, you sleep yet?" He said with excitement. "Look out the window!"

"No thanks."

"Check out the view" he said in awe. Is it me or is he forgetting that we were on the flight to Hawaii together.

"I saw it already." I replied.

My attitude is obvious but he's too excited to care. I am tired, hungry and now annoyed. No, I am starving and we just had breakfast. Nine more hours with no food? I'm gonna die! Andrew better leave me alone.

When I finally woke up we were landing. I am so ready to talk to Jodi and get to the bottom of this texting situation. We got into the Uber Andrew called, and sat in silence. Back to reality, and reality is I don't have to tiptoe around shit anymore. I am going to find out what is going on. I texted Jodi to schedule our appointment.

5:16pm Sent: "Hi Jodi, I hope all is well. I'm back from Hawaii, are you available Monday"

5:17pm Received: "Yes! Welcome Back! Same Time?"

Wow, that was fast. At least someone misses me.

5:20pm Sent: "Yes, mam! See you soon."

5:23pm Received: "Great!"

What I can't figure out is, am I attracting these bad situations? I thought that it was finally my time to be with a good one. I thought Andrew finally changed. Maybe no one really ever changes? Or maybe, i've been so paranoid that I just over think and manifest. Although for the most part I think positive, I'm not ... well, not that I am not, I mean ... I don't mean to think about the negative, but it happens. I'm Human.

We pulled up at my mother's house and Andrew unloaded our bags from the Uber. He walked over to our car in my mother's driveway and loaded them in the trunk. I walked over to the door and rang the bell. I heard little feet approaching the door.

"Mommy!" Steve yelled.

"Daddy!" He yelled again!

"How are you guys? I've missed you so much!" I picked Steven up into my arms and Tahj ran over to Drew.

"Hey Pop!"

"Hey Tahj!" he responded tossing him in the air.

"Hey mom!" I yelled to my mother.

"Tahj was teaching me!" Steve explained. "Yeah?" I asked.

"Yeah, he taught me the game" he continued.

"Oh! Okay, good job Tahj."

"Thanks mommy" he smirked.

I walked into my mother's kitchen and she was putting food in a take home dish.

"They ate already, but I am sure Kenzie is not in the mood for cooking after that long flight."

"You are absolutely right" I responded to my mother before giving her a kiss on the cheek.

I snuck a piece of fried chicken and quickly walked away. Her chicken was like no other, she specialized in chicken wings and baked mac and cheese.

"We have to go back as a family ma, it was amazing" Drew told my mother.

"Yeah, we can make that happen" she responded.

"Let's go boys, mommy is tired."

"You're still tired?" Drew asked me with confusion.

"Tahj, let's go!" Steven yelled running over to me."

Tahj was busy making sure there was no toy left behind. We said our goodbyes and went outside to get into the car. The drive home was the exact opposite experience from the drive to my moms. Loud. The boys were so excited to see us, it was like they had a million and one things to tell us about.

I cannot wait to see Jodi. The things I could say to Drew right now ... I'll just wait before I do or say something I may regret. But, come on now on our honeymoon? Who does that? Who is this bitch? Everyone knows we are married now.

When we got home I headed inside with Steven and

Tahj while Andrew unloaded the car. They went to their room and I went to my bed.

"I'm still surprised that you are still tired." Andrew said as he walked in with our bags.

"Yup, a quick nap will do." I responded.

When I woke up I looked to my right and Andrew was knocked out. Mouth wide open, snoring really loud and spread out like a baby. I got up and headed towards the boys room. Sometimes Steve is up late, usually we both are. Tahj can't hang and neither can Andrew.

I looked at the clock on the wall once I got to their room. It read 4:47am. I am glad he is asleep, waking up in the morning would have been a struggle.
After leaving the boys room I went into the kitchen to grab some grapes, my favorite fruit. I got a bowl out of the drain board and filled it with grapes and walked over to my desk. It'll be nice to get a journal entry in before I get tired again.

4:56am   August 20, 2016
There is never a dull moment in my life. Prior to our wedding I ran into Trent at the bar on Brooklawn in Bridgeport. Although we live in Hamden, a lot of our friends are from Bridgeport so we still travel back and forth. I was meeting Lily for drinks and wings at Nineteenth. He was in there sitting at the bar wit his face all sad like a puppy. He proceeded to tell us about his new life, his new kids and how he is still not happy. Typical Trent. He was never happy! I could not make him happy, there was something wrong with me or what I was doing at all times. Anyway though, on our honeymoon I was in the bathroom and Andrew's phone was on the charger one morning. His phone lit up because he received a text message. Someone said they couldn't wait to see him . . . why do people always try me? Do I have FUCK

WITH ME written on my forehead? I'm trying my hardest to be a better person, but I am not and will not tolerate bullshit. We are an official family now, I don't play with mine.

Kenz

    I got up from my desk and went to the kitchen, turned the light over the oven on and turned off the rest of the lights. I tried to quietly get back in bed but someone was already awake so it didn't matter.

    "Can't sleep?" Andrew said. He pulled me close and kissed me on my back. "We have church in the morning remember, try to get some more rest." He continued. I shook my head and fell back asleep.

    Sunday seem to have come and gone. The pastors message was about marriage and building a family. How ironic! The bible verse he quoted "*For husbands, this means love your wives, just as Christ loved the church. He gave up his life for her.*" Came from **Ephesians 5:25**, it spoke to me but I wonder did that resonate with him. After church I didn't do too much besides sleep and eat while Andrew took the boys to the park. Before they came back into the house for dinner I had already fallen asleep for the night.

    "Good Morning Mommy!" Steven said tugging on my harm.

    "Good Morning, how are you?" I asked him mid yawn.

    "Good! Tahj awake too."

    "Oh? Where is he?" I asked, I'm still so impressed with the way Steven speaks at only two years old.

    "Hey Mom, I'm right here." He was at the bottom of my bed looking at me.

    "Oh, Good Morning Baby! I got up and kissed the both of them.

    "Let's get ready for camp." I took both of them by

their hands and went to the bathroom. I put them both in the bath after running their water. While they played, I brushed my teeth.

"I'm ready mom" Tahj said first. He stood up so that I can wash him. When I was done with Tahj it was Steven's turn and he knew it. My baby boy jumped up and gave me his wash cloth. He shook his little booty while singing " my turn, my turn!"

I laughed and proceeded to wash Victor.

"Daddy left?" he asked.

"No, he's in the bed" I wrapped Steven in his towel and whispered. "Go wake him up."

I smiled as his face lit up and he began to yell and run down the hall.

"Daddy! Mommy said to wake you up!" Tahj was brushing his teeth and by the time Steven got to the end of the hall, he was finishing up.

"Are my clothes ready?" He asked.

"No, I'll go pick out your clothes. I'm sorry, come on." I took him by his hand and went to his room.

"Were you sleeping a lot and forgot to take out my clothes?" Tahj asked.

"Yes. I'm really tired."

"Are you pregnant again?" Tahj continued. I stopped what I was doing and asked him to repeat himself.

"Am In trouble?" He asked.

"Oh, No sweetie. Did you ask if I was pregnant again?" Tahj shook his head yes.

"Well, what made you ask me that?"

"I don't know just asking." He responded blushing.

Tahj told me I was pregnant in his own way when I was pregnant with Steven. But, I doubt I am pregnant this time.

"Do you want another brother or sister?" I inquired.

"A sister would be nice, I already have Steven and JJ."

He explained.

Jake Jr and Tahj are the same age.

"I'm going to let you get dressed. I'm going to get in the shower." I kissed him on the forehead and walked away. I ran my water and got into the shower. By the time I was done, Andrew was coming in to brush his teeth.

"Hey Bae?"

"Hmm?" I replied while drying off.

"Are you dropping them?"

"I can." I responded

"Okay, Tahj is putting his shoes on and Steven is already dressed."

"Wow that was fast." I said in amazement.

"You know me." He responded with a smirk.

I brushed my teeth after he was done and headed to my bedroom to get dressed.

"Hi mommy! Does your breath still stink?" I burst out laughing after hearing Steven behind me.

"You-Tell- Me! Come over here and give me kisses." He giggled and ran into my arms.

"I love you mommy" he said laying his head on my shoulder.

"I love you too lil' baby! Go get your brother, tell him it's time to go."

"Time to go?" He reiterated.

I shook my head yes "Okay, time to go Tahj!! It's time to go! Come on!" he yelled running out of my room and down the hall.

Once I was done getting dressed I said my goodbyes to Drew and headed to the car with the boys. Their camp was down the street from our home and Jodi's office wasn't too far either. I walked them into camp and drove a few more minutes to my session.

I parked and walked into the office building. There was an unfamiliar face sitting at the receptionist desk.

"Hello, my name is McKenzie Perkins. I'm here to see Jodi Williams." I introduced myself before signing into the log-in book.

"Hello, my name is Rebecca. I'm filling in for Tori." Rebecca extended her hand for a handshake.

"Nice to meet you Rebecca."

"The pleasure is mine; I will let Jodi know you are here."

Rebecca made a call to Jodi and a few minutes later she told me I can go in to see her.

"Hey McKenzie! How are you, newly wed?" Jodi said with excitement as she came over and hugged me.

"I'm well! I'm doing well."

"That's it?" Jodi stepped back with a frown. "You should be extremely excited."

"I can't seem ... to be happy. Something is always in the way."

"Are you giving that 'something' or 'someone' too much power? It is controlling your emotions and I don't have to tell you that, that isn't healthy." She responded.

"Well, uh. So, Andrew received a text message on his phone from a female stating she couldn't wait to see him." I explained.

"Well, how do you know it was a female?" Jodi asked with sass.

"Well, the person said they couldn't wait to see him." Jodi's face went from sarcastic to a perplexed facial expression after my response.

"Yeah" I continued "So, no I don't want to give this situation power but...it is what it is."

I really do feel like I am manifesting these bad situations and it's obviously not on purpose. Who does that?

"On another note, to avoid giving that situation "power" I continued with air quotes and emphasis on power. "I saw my ex Trent! I dated him prior to getting back with

Andrew."

"How did that go?" Jodi asked. She picked up her cup took a sip and picked up her pen and notepad.

"It was awkward. He was at a bar and me and my best friend walked in. He looked so sad so we indulged in some conversation. He began to tell me how he was unhappy with his life because he could not live his dreams and run his businesses. He said that he wished things ended differently between the two of us so that we could continue to motivate each other." I explained.

I guess his new girl doesn't give him any. Any motivation, I mean.

"So, tell me about Trent."

"Trent was nice; he treated me to nice things. Initially, I think I was attracted to him because he looked like a celebrity I had a crush on. Plus, he was older and I liked a challenge. Trent always made it clear he didn't want marriage and he didn't want any children. This actually caused me to keep him and Tahj apart if I could help it. That should have been the first sign but nope, not for me. I'm not that smart clearly... but anyway. He helped me buy my second car and pushed me to start my real estate career. He was great in that aspect, we could have made a lot of money together. We were probably better off business partners."

"How did you meet him?"

"Oh, he was my boss; I worked for him at a restaurant. "I explained.

"Your boss" She reiterated.

"My boss" I smiled.

"You are full of surprises, but that was also another sign." Jodi responded. "But, continue. What happened with him? How did you guys end?"

"He used to talk to me like I was his child instead of his girlfriend. The same guy who never wanted any kids thought he had one when it came to me. I was 19 years old and he was 27, so granted he was 8 years older than me but still it is not okay." I carried on. "He used to tell me I didn't know anything and if I did something he didn't agree with he'd use his three favorite words. I was either: dumb, stupid or retarded."

Jodi shook her head as if she thought I was crazy.

"He told me I was fat. I was only 130 pounds and I had just had Tahj the only fat on me was the little bit of stomach I had. I always had a fear of gaining too much weight so it wasn't until then that I got the point. I knew it was time for me to go. He was so, disgusted when it came to my weight and how he described me being discombobulated. He had an entire beer belly with a messy beard." I began to show Jodi how big Trent's belly was and she started laughing.

"Do you want to know what his new girl looks like?" I laughed out loud.

"No! Be nice" she continued to laugh.

On a serious note though, Trent used to hurt my feelings with the weight comments and he really didn't care. It sucked. It felt like being with Jake again, except emotionally.

"Okay, let's get serious now. That is a form of bullying. And it is not healthy. I'm glad that you left him and I hope he finds peace."

"Maybe he should come see you" I chuckled.

"Maybe?" Jodi laughed "It seems like sometimes you do know when to let go of people. You knew it was time to start over with Trent versus the situation with Jamar. What was different?"

"There was not a long drawn out history, and I actually tried my best. I tried to make him happy, I tried to be an adult before I was even actually a real one. With Jamar, I tried but I was still curious about how it could turn out to be. With Trent, I did not care to find out anymore because no matter what he was only happy for five minutes and he started to attack my weight. I just knew it was over." I answered Jodi.

"You know I have some homework for you right?" She laughed

"Of course you do!"

"Journal about how you feel when you think about your past with Trent. When you are done, rip it out and throw it in the trash. Close that chapter."

"Will do." I nodded my head up and down.

"Now, Back to your husband. Andrew received a text message? Were you going through his phone?" Jodi assumed.

"No. It lit up while I was in the bathroom, and I took a peek" I said while flashing an innocent smile.

"Okay, so earlier you mentioned it was a female. Who do you think it is?"

"His ex-girlfriend possibly. Her name is Tammy."

"Why did she come to mind? Tell me about Tammy." She responded while sitting back.

Non-Factor:

Andrew was a basketball player, a pretty popular one since I've known him. He wasn't really into begging for female attention or if he was I didn't know about it because he kept his business private. We dated in middle school and ended up in the same high school. He had a few girlfriends but one in particular he stayed with for some years. Tammy.

"Tammy and Andrew dated for about two or three years in high school. Tammy was so beautiful back then. She had the perfect video girl body that everyone wanted at the time; slim up top, thick at the bottom. We had plenty of mutual friends but she and I were not friends at all. Her attitude was horrible and I always had a thing for Andrew so I didn't like her out the gate." I explained to Jodi.

"I used to hug him a little tighter than usual when she was around just to see her upset." I continued "Fast forward to after graduating high school, they dated a bit longer on and off. The same year they broke up for good we got back together. So, I can definitely understand the attachment because maybe the door was never really closed prior to us jumping back in. Maybe, she thought I was temporary. Maybe, she thought she could run me away. I don't scare easy and I like challenges. Plus, the drama that they brought didn't touch the surface compared to my drama with Jamar."

"Go on" Jodi chuckled.

"For a while, prior to us getting what I would call "serious"; I didn't mind him talking to her or seeing her or whatever because I was doing my own thing too."

"What does whatever mean? Be specific." Jodi asked.

"Well, I didn't mind if he was having sex with her, that's what I meant by whatever."

"hmm, go on." Jodi said as she made a note in her

notepad.

"She used to post little stupid subliminal messages about them still being friends because she thought that I wasn't aware. She used to say the craziest things for attention, not knowing that she can't bother someone who is already in the loop. I had a conversation with her over the phone to let her know we were living together. She thought she was dropping bombs on me by telling me certain things again, not knowing that I already knew." I explained to Jodi "She was soooooo dramatic, it was ridiculous. I thought I was done with crazy, until I seen that text."

"Well, how do you know it's her?" Jodi asked.
"I am almost positive, everyone else knows and respects the relationship. Everyone except her, she doesn't mind sharing him as long as she has a piece."

Jodi nodded her head prior to responding.

"Here is homework." She said as she sat up in her seat. "Write down three things you can do to let Tammy go."

"What does that mean?" I said with a sarcastic tone.

"Well, you have been holding on to this situation for a while. Clearly. You have to let it go so that you can move on from it. Communication and trust is a big part of your growth. Ask him if it's —"

I usually have my phone on silent but I forgot today. It rang loudly and interrupted Jodi's comment.

"I apologize, what were you saying?"

"Simply ask him and respect his answer." She continued as my phone went off again.

"I'm sorry, it's Andrew. Do you mind? I asked Jodi for permission to answer the phone.

"No! Of course not." She responded with a smile.

"Where are you Kenz? I called you twice." He yelled on the other end of the phone.

"I'm still at therapy whats up Drew? What's wrong?"

"Well, your new truck was delivered this morning with

the bow on it. I found your pregnancy test yesterday and figured you would need an upgrade." He explained.

My Jaw dropped. "Did you go through the trash? And who's the girl that texted you saying she couldn't wait to see you." I retorted.

"Oh, so that's what the attitude was about. It was my mother. She got a new phone number and I forgot to save it. I guess we haven't gotten past the past huh? See you soon." He finished before hanging up.

"So, did he answer?" Jodi asked.

"It was his mother" I said as I burst into laughter. "I guess Tammy is still a non-factor."

Jodi looked at me with the straightest face ever. "Do you see what happens when you ask a simple question McKenzie?" she began to laugh "let that be a lesson learned."

"You're right, and um he bought me a new car because he found my pregnancy test in the trash." I blushed.

"You like to end your sessions with a bang huh? Congratulations McKenzie!!!!! Oh WOW! How do you feel?"

"I feel much lighter now that I know it was just his mother, now I can have my baby in peace." I laughed.

"Cut him some slack. You're growing, he's growing. You're ending the cycle that you created years ago. The first step was you coming here, moving forward we can continue to talk it out and you should continue to journal and release those feelings on paper. It's one thing to feel a way but don't let it take over your day to day life. Despite what you felt with the people from your past you have a family who loves you and a bright future with them. Do not ruin that, you are perfect just the way you are for them and your new baby."

"Yes Jodi!! I will strive to create better experiences in my life. I'll focus on good and when I'm feeling down I will do what you said and release it on paper." I responded.

"Good. Now, what are we hoping for?" She asked while

smiling from ear to ear.

"A girl, we already have a boy and he's raising Jake's son as his own so all we need is a girl."

"I figured Tahj's biological father was Jake, but I was waiting for you to say it without my assumption." Jodi said matter-a-factly. Well, I'll hope for a girl with you! Give me a hug before you go. Next time we will have a normal session but go check out your new truck and thank your husband."

I got up to give Jodi a hug. "Okay Jodi, thank you so much. I will see you soon!! I'm going to get my keys!! Ha ha" I exclaimed as I headed out the door.

I waived bye to Rebecca and ran to my car. It felt like I was driving for five minutes the way I sped home. Andrew had two champagne flutes in his hand when I arrived. I hoped out and ran to give him a big hug. My truck was the Range Rover Sport I've been dying for. The color was black and white with a red bow on the hood. Andrew passed me my champagne flute and smiled.

"It's sparkling Cider" he raised his glass.

"To us" he continued.

"To us" I responded before we kissed.

www.ingramcontent.com/pod-product-compliance
Lightning Source LLC
Chambersburg PA
CBHW070549300426
44113CB00011B/1834